CELTIC WARRIORS

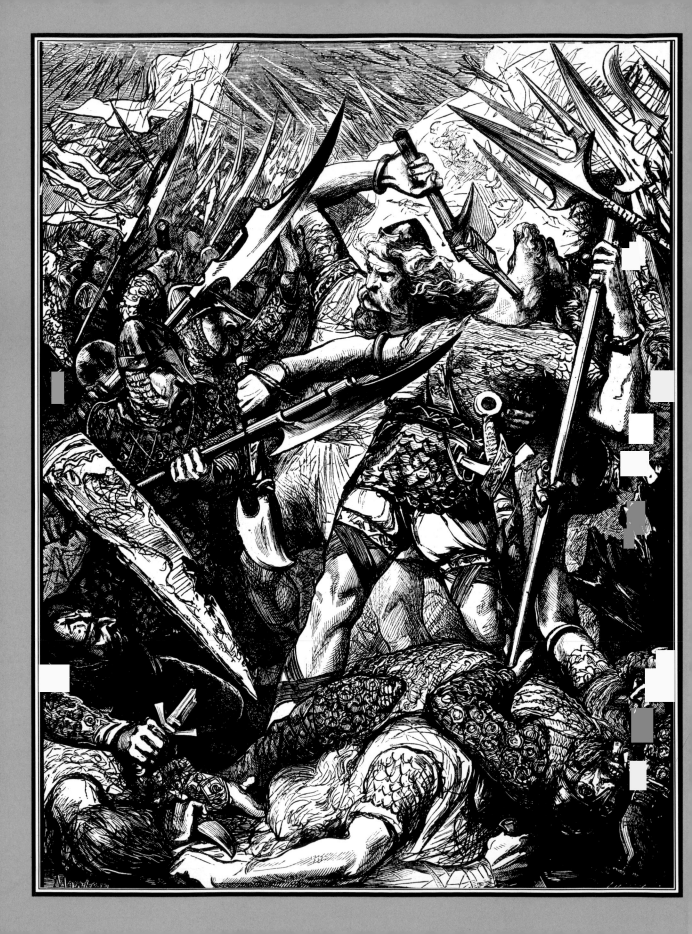

CELTIC WARRIORS

400 BC – 1600 AD
TIM NEWARK

COLOUR ILLUSTRATIONS
BY ANGUS McBRIDE

BLANDFORD

For my mother

First published in the UK 1986 by Blandford Press
Villiers House, 41-47 Strand
London WC2N 5JE,
a Cassell Company.

This paperback edition published in 1988

Reprinted 1990, 1991, 1992, 1993

Copyright © 1986 Blandford Press Ltd.
Text copyright © 1986 Tim Newark

Distributed in the United States by
Sterling Publishing Co, Inc,
387 Park Avenue South, New York, NY 10016-8810

Distributed in Australia by
Capricorn Link (Australia) Pty Ltd
PO Box 665, Lane Cove, NSW 2066

British Library Cataloguing in Publication Data

Newark, Tim
  Celtic warriors: 400 BC–1600.
  1. Celts—History
  2. Europe—History, Military
  I. Title
  940′.04916   D25.5

ISBN 0-7137-2043-3

Typeset by Graphicraft Hong Kong
Printed and bound in Hong Kong by Colorcraft Ltd.

Contents

Preface

At one time, the Celts dominated the ancient world from Spain to Turkey. They sacked Rome and invaded Greece. Their war chariots devastated all adversaries. But then it all went wrong. They were crushed by the Roman Empire. Their legendary kingdoms in Europe were no more. Only Britain remained a Celtic stronghold. And even there, the Scots, the Welsh, and the Irish were forced to fight for their independence against waves of Anglo-Saxons, Vikings, and Anglo-Normans.

This book tells the heroic story of two thousand years of Celtic warfare. From four centuries before Christ to the sixteenth century, it describes the dramatic, hard-fought withdrawal before succeeding military powers and the times when the Celts struck back. It celebrates the persistent struggle of the Celtic-speaking people to retain their independence and their way of life. The occasions of unity and the defeat brought by division.

As a survey, this book serves as an introduction to Celtic military culture and it is hoped will encourage reading in depth to discover further the true character of the Celtic warrior.

Tim Newark 1985

The Golden Age

When Alexander the Great asked an envoy of Celtic warriors what they feared most, he expected them to say 'You, my lord.' Instead they replied: 'We fear only that the sky fall and crush us, or the earth open and swallow us, or the sea rise and overwhelm us.' A peace was made, but Alexander was furious. How dare a tribe of insignificant barbarians fear the fantastic more than his realistic military might. Fifty years later, this same confident people devastated Alexander's homeland of Macedonia.

The raiding campaign of 279 BC was an ambitious one for the Celts. Living north of the Danube, they had pillaged Thrace and Macedonia before. But this time they had killed the King of Macedonia, heir to the glory of Alexander and Philip. A fever of adventure gripped the army of raiders. This expedition would be different. Brennus, their chieftain, described the rich townships of Greece. He told his followers of the sacred sanctuaries crammed with gold and silver offerings to the Greek gods. He knew it was a good time to embark on such a campaign. The Macedonian Empire had broken up: the Greeks were a divided people. The Celts mounted their horses and rode south.

Tales of Celtic atrocities in Thessaly gradually convinced many Greeks to forget their wrangling and combine their forces. They chose to confront the Celtic warriors at Thermopylae. Almost exactly two hundred years earlier, a Greek army had fought a bitter last stand at this mountain pass against Persian invaders. The tragic outcome of that gallant defence of their homeland cannot have escaped those Greeks now guarding the narrow

9

mountain roads. In order to prevent the Celts even reaching Thermopylae, Callippus, the Athenian commander of the Greek force, sent a detachment of horsemen to the river Spercheius. There they broke down all the bridges across the fast-running waters.

Unhindered by any major resistance, Brennus had led his warriors along the coast. Having come so far, the Celts would not be denied their booty. That same night as the Greeks camped on the bankside, a group of Celtic raiders crossed the Spercheius lower down, in slower waters. Swimming in the dark, they used their long shields as rafts. Next morning, the Greeks dashed back to Thermopylae while Brennus forced the local population to rebuild the bridges. Needing food and supplies and in no rush to confront the Greek army, the Celts were content to plunder the countryside around Heracleia. They did not even bother to attack the town. But the Greek army mustering at Thermopylae could not be avoided indefinitely. Celtic scouts and Greek deserters warned Brennus that it increased day by day.

On the day of conflict, it was the Greeks who began the battle. At sunrise they advanced quietly and in good order. Because of the rough terrain and the many streams that hurtled down the mountainside, horsemen proved useless and the majority of fighting was on foot. Despite being unarmoured except for their shields, the Celts fought with impressive ferocity. Some drew out from their wounds the spears by which they had been hit and threw them back at the Greeks. As the battle for the pass raged, the Athenian contingent rowed their triremes along the coast of Thermopylae: a coastline slowly silting up and becoming a salt-marsh. They attacked the flank of the Celts with arrows and slingshot. The Celts were hard pressed and many fell into the swamp, sinking beneath the mud. The first day of battle ended with many losses.

After a week's rest, Brennus decided to split his enemy's ranks. He sent horsemen off to the neighbouring region of Aetolia. Their plundering soon reached the ears of the Aetolian warriors camped at Thermopylae. Desperately worried by this assault on their homeland, they immediately left their Greek allies and pursued the Celtic raiders. Brennus now capitalised on the resentment of local Greeks. Fed up with the freebooters on their soil, local herdsmen were happy to see the Celts clear off along the many remote mountain paths. Acting as guides, they led Brennus and his warriors along the same tracks that had allowed the Persians to outflank the Greeks.

Obscured by a morning mist, Celtic warriors suddenly descended on the Greek guards of the mountain pass. Fighting a fierce rear-guard, the majority of the Greeks managed to clamber into Athenian ships and were evacuated from certain disaster. Thermopylae, however, belonged to the Celts and they now pressed on southwards through the mountains. The Celts had been promised the treasures of the Greek temples. But, as they approached the sacred territory of Delphi, it seemed that the very gods of the Greeks had finally rallied to protect their own people. Earthquakes shuddered beneath the raiders. Great rocks tumbled down from Mount

Bronze spearhead found in a burial mound at Snowshill, Gloucestershire, England. Early Bronze Age. The makers of this blade were a proto-Celtic people from central Europe who used their metal-working skills to spread their areas of influence and trade throughout western Europe. Their established routes of conquest were followed by later Celtic communities.

Bronze tanged and socketed spearheads found at Arreton Down, Isle of Wight, England. Early Bronze Age, 1600–1400 BC, now in the British Museum, London. Such keen-bladed weapons gave these warriors a significant advantage over the prehistoric natives of the lands they dominated.

Parnassus and bottomless crags ripped open. Thunder crashed all around. Lightning bolts engulfed individual warriors in heavenly fire. Amidst the chaos, the weird shapes of the ghosts of past Greek heroes arose.

As Delphi came within view, the supernatural forces were joined by the very real strength of a Greek army. To this were added the guerilla assaults of the local Phocians, haunting the snow-covered slopes of Mount Parnassus and pouring arrows and javelins into the Celtic ranks. In the face of all this, the Celtic warriors fought remarkably well. But that night, battered

11

and exhausted, a panic spread through their camp. In the dark, thinking they were being attacked by the Greeks, Celt killed Celt. The next day, Greek reinforcements chased the Celts back to Heracleia. During the long retreat, Brennus, already wounded, took his own life. Harried throughout Thessaly, few of the Celtic raiders returned home.

This then is the legend of the Celtic raid on Greece in 279 BC as recorded by Pausanias, a Greek historian of the second century AD. Analysing his account, one is immediately aware of several discrepancies and clichés. The Celtic raid on Delphi did not fall short of the city and end in a dismal rout. The Roman historian Livy writes several times of the pillage of Delphi while Strabo even suggests that treasure found in the sacred Celtic lake at Toulouse originated from Delphi. Moreover, after satisfying themselves in Greece, the Celts advanced back along the coast to the wealthy port of Byzantium where they crossed into Asia Minor. There they fought as mercenaries for the King of Bithynia. They then advanced further into Turkey and established themselves in territory belonging to the Phrygians, around present-day Ankara. The lands became known as Galatia and the descendants of those Celtic warriors continued to terrorise Asia Minor for over a hundred years, extracting tributes from rulers as far away as Syria.

Pausanias is guilty also of cultural cliché. His vision of the Celts is one of badly-armed, near-naked savages. Of course, he admits, they fight courageously but it is the ferocity of animals. When confronted by the cool discipline of Greek warriors, these yelping, charging wildmen have to resort to the sneaky subterfuge of the barbarian Persians: a stratagem facilitated by Greek traitors. However, even Pausanias has to admit that Brennus—for a barbarian—handled the crossing of the river Spercheius with efficiency and success. But, like all Imperialist correspondents, Pausanias greatly exaggerates the numbers of the raging savages: 200,000 Celts against 25,000 Greeks.

In reality, the Celtic force that invaded Greece was probably little stronger than those raiding parties which frequently crossed the Danube. Along the way, it may have been joined by Greek bandits but it cannot have been more than a few thousand. It would also have been divided up into numerous plundering gangs, scattered across the countryside, not at all suited to a pitched battle. Such warriors were professional raiders and augmented their own arms with a variety of stolen armour and weapons. They were better equipped and of a higher morale than the hastily assembled Greek forces that confronted them. The oldest specimen of interlinked mail yet found has been excavated from a third-century BC Celtic grave in Romania and this was probably developed from protective garments made up of rings threaded onto cords, like netting; a fragment of which has been found in an eighth-century Halstatt grave in Bohemia.

The renowned ferocity of the Celts was not all Greek myth. Livy puts a vivid description of the Galatians into the speech of Gnaeus Manlius Volso, a consul sent to crush the Asian Celts in 189 BC. 'They sing as they advance into battle,' the consul warns his troops, 'they yell and leap in the air, clashing their weapons against their shields. The Greeks and Phrygians are scared by this display, but the Romans are used to such wildness. We have learned that if you can bear up to their first onslaught—that initial charge of blind passion—then their limbs will grow weary with the effort and when their passion subsides, they are overcome by sun, dust, and thirst. And anyway, these Celts we face are of a mixed blood, part Greek. Not the Gauls our forefathers fought.' Despite references to the 'degeneracy' of the Galatians, such a description of the Galatians differs little from other

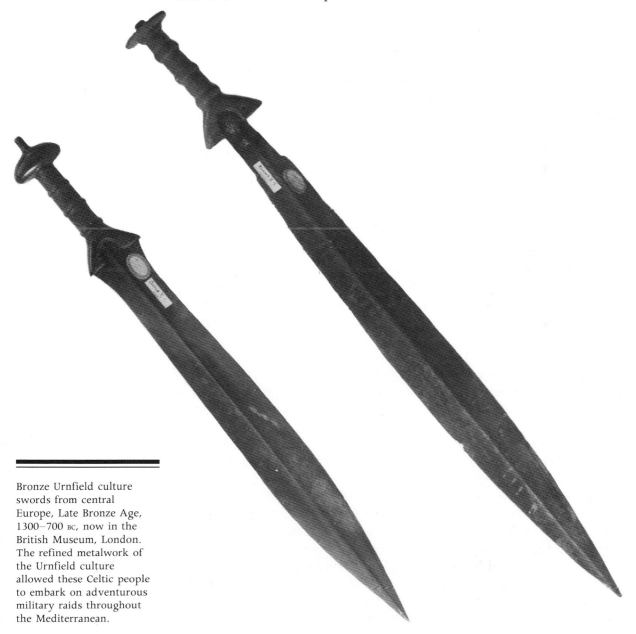

Bronze Urnfield culture swords from central Europe, Late Bronze Age, 1300–700 BC, now in the British Museum, London. The refined metalwork of the Urnfield culture allowed these Celtic people to embark on adventurous military raids throughout the Mediterranean.

13

accounts of Celtic and Germanic warriors in Europe. Here again, the ferocity of the Celts is respected, but it is undermined by a lack of discipline and staying power which the Romans can turn to their advantage.

Such a vision of the Celts as ferocious barbarians has endured over the centuries. In the culture war of projected images, the Celts have come off second best to Graeco-Roman propaganda. This is largely because the Celtic peoples of central Europe maintained a culture without writing. The only written accounts we have of them in the thousand years until the fifth century AD are Greek and Latin. We see the Celts through the eyes of their enemies: it is like writing a history of twentieth-century America based on Russian chronicles. Aspects of the Celts were admired, but at best they are represented as noble savages cowed by the might of classical civilization. It is a tradition mirrored in Mediterranean art. When King Attalus I of Pergamum defeated a force of Galatians in around 230 BC, he commemorated his victory with a series of sculpture. In actual fact, the victory was short-lived and the Galatians continued powerful until the next century, but the Pergamene sculptures of defeated Gauls were copied throughout the Greek and Roman world.

The most famous of these images, *The Dying Gaul*, shows a naked Celtic warrior kneeling wounded and subdued on his shield. Only the Celtic torque round his neck suggests the strength that had to be conquered to render this figure pathetic. A Roman marble copy of this sculpture now stands in the Capitoline Museum in Rome to remind us all continually of the defeated Celtic people: supposedly a naked, savage race inevitably overwhelmed by the higher civilization of the Mediterranean. Another sculpture copied from the Pergamum group, now also in Rome, shows again a Celt with characteristic wild hair and moustache (Romans and Greeks never wore moustaches without beards). This time the figure has slain his wife and is stabbing himself in the chest rather than be taken alive. A gallant and brave but eventual loser. Just as the Romans wanted them.

The true standing and culture of the pre-literate Celts can only be deduced from archaelogical discoveries. That they emerge as a recognisable collection of tribes in the first millenium BC is revealed by a series of finds in central Europe. These consist predominantly of bronze and iron metalwork and their famous hill-fort settlements. The people were called *Keltoi* by the Greeks and *Galli* by the Romans. That all these peoples of central Europe were called Celts is because from the fifth century BC onwards they were identified as speaking variations of the same Celtic tongue: an Indo-European language distinct from that of the Germans and the people of the Mediterranean, and now surviving only in the language of the Gaelic Irish and Scots, the Welsh and the Bretons.

The ancient Celts were not a unified people. They did not rule an All-Celtic Empire. Their many hill-forts attest to the fact that Celtic tribes throughout Europe fought and raided against each other as much as they did against the Romans, Greeks and Germans. Nevertheless, archaeological finds maintain that they did share a similar culture as well as a common language. That they did not develop the art of writing does not mean that this culture was any inferior to that of the Romans or Greeks. Technologically and economically, they were equal to their southern neighbours and in peace a thriving trade was continued between them. As an alternative to literature, the Celts developed highly skilled patterns of speech. Their verbal eloquence was valued and respected not only by themselves but also by the Romans and other literate races. Without doubt, however, it was the Celtic lack of written records that contributed to their apparent and real decline in influence and power from the third century BC onwards. Indeed, it is remarkable that the Celts retained any of their potent presence in European history in the face of Latin culture and warfare.

Before the Roman war-machine reached its zenith, the Celts enjoyed a golden age of martial prowess. From a heartland in central Europe, Celtic warriors carried their culture and influence into France, Spain, and Britain. Native tribesmen were unable to resist their long iron swords. By the fifth century BC, the Celts had overcome the Etruscans in northern Italy and settled the land of the river Po. In 390 BC Rome was sacked and several Roman armies humbled. Why were these Celtic warriors so successful? We are told they were fierce fighters. But, above everything else, they were horse-warriors—superb horse-warriors. So renowned were they that they were employed as mercenary cavalry by Greeks and Romans throughout antiquity. Strabo states that the Celts were better horsemen than foot-soldiers and the best mercenary cavalry the Romans ever employed: a recommendation echoed by Caesar, who almost exclusively used Celtic horsemen in his Gallic campaigns.

One of the earliest accounts of Celtic horsemanship to survive is recorded by Xenophon, a Greek historian and cavalry officer of the fourth century BC. In the war between Sparta and Thebes, he records, mercenary troops were sent by Dionysius of Syracuse to aid the Spartans. Xenophon's text makes a distinction between the Celts, Iberians, and horsemen sent, but this seems a later manuscript error and they are all one and the same: Celtic or Celtiberian horse-warriors. Xenophon describes their performance against a Theban army plundering a plain near Corinth. 'Few though they were,' he wrote, 'they were scattered here and there. They charged towards the Thebans, threw their javelins, and then dashed away as the enemy moved towards them, often turning around and throwing more javelins. While pursuing these tactics, they sometimes dismounted for a rest. But if anyone charged upon them while they were resting, they would easily leap onto their horses and retreat. If enemy warriors pursued them far from the Theban army, these horsemen would then turn around and wrack them with their javelins. Thus they manipulated the entire Theban army, compelling it to advance or fall back at their will.' Xenophon is a trustworthy chronicler of military horsemanship as he was himself a cavalry officer and wrote a treatise on the subject. Later, in his account of

Bronze ornamented mace-
heads from southern
Germany, now in the State
Prehistorical Collection,
Munich. Urnfield culture,
late Bronze Age, 1250–750 BC.

Bronze antennae-hilted sword. No provenance, but probably from Urnfield groups in central Europe, now in the British Museum, London. Late Bronze Age, 1300–700 BC.

Greek wars of the 360s, he gives an example of how horsemen are best used in battle. As a force of Arcadians give way to the Spartans, a group of Celtic horsemen are sent after the fleeing Greeks, cutting down the running foot-soldiers.

Five hundred years later, Pausanias gave an equally vivid and interesting account of Celtic horsemen. 'To each horseman were attached two servants, he wrote. 'These were themselves skilled riders and each had a horse. When the horse-warriors were engaged in combat, the servants remained behind. However, should a horse fall, then a servant brought a new horse for the warrior to mount. And if the warrior were killed, a servant mounted the horse in his master's place. If both rider and horse were hurt then one servant would ride out to replace him, while another led the wounded warrior back to camp. Thus the Celts kept up their strength throughout a battle.' This description may have been based on earlier chroniclers nearer the time of the Celtic invasion of Greece, or it may have been inspired by contemporary Celtic horsemanship in the second century AD. Whatever its source, it clearly demonstrates a sophisticated use of cavalry. It shows that Celtic horsemen possessed a high social and economic status like that of a medieval knight in relation to his squire and attendants. It suggests that Celtic horsemen fought in military units similar to the medieval 'lance' in which a heavily armed horse-warrior was supported by lighter cavalrymen who were also grooms.

The power and importance of the Celtic horse and rider is dynamically represented in Celtic art. From the great white horses carved into the chalk slopes of southern England to the tiny representations of horse-warriors on Celtic gold coins: both are symbols of dominance over the native population and the means by which it was achieved. As to the horse equipment itself, much ingenuity and craftsmanship was lavished on it. Sophisticated flexible iron horse bits from France have been dated from the fifth to the third centuries BC. In Scotland is preserved a fascinating piece of bronze armour for a horse's head. It is magnificently decorated with swirling patterns and has two curved horns attached to it. As in most societies, it appears that horsemanship was predominantly the preserve of aristocratic, wealthy warriors. An intriguing glimpse of what an ancient Celtic horse-warrior may have looked like in all his finery is provided by a relief on the Gundestrup Cauldron.

Found in a Danish peat-bog and dated to the second century BC, the cauldron depicts Celtic warriors of central Europe. The horsemen wear short, tight-fitting linen tunics. Some may also have worn the knee-length trousers of the foot-soldiers lined up beneath them. On their heads, the horsemen wear iron helmets with elaborate bird and boar crests. According to the head decorations on the Aylesford bucket, some helmets also had huge curled horns. The horsemen wear spurs but, of course, no stirrups. Bridle and harness are decorated with metal plates. Chieftains and noble soldiers probably also wore torques around their necks and shirts of mail.

17

On the Gundestrup Cauldron, the horse-warriors are clearly in command, wearing the most expensive arms. Beneath them are foot-soldiers armed only with spears and large rectangular shields. They wear no helmets. At the end of the line of foot-soldiers is a warrior wearing a helmet with boar's head crest. He presumably belongs to the same class as the horse-warriors and is some kind of officer. Behind him are three foot-soldiers blowing on long trumpets shaped like a horse's head. This is the clearest Celtic record we have of the composition of an ancient Celtic army.

The excellence of Celtic horsemanship extended to their famous use of chariots. 'The chariots of the Britons,' wrote Julius Caesar, 'begin the fighting by charging over the battlefield. From them they hurl javelins; although the noise of the wheels and chariot teams are enough to throw any enemy into panic. The charioteers are very skilled. They can drive their teams down very steep slopes without losing control. Some warriors can run along the chariot pole, stand on the yoke and then dart back into the chariot.' Primarily, it seems, Celtic chariots were for display, intended to overawe and enemy in the prelude to battle. Once involved in combat—according to Caesar and Diodorus of Sicily—a chariot team would dismount to fight, using it more as a means of fast retreat or advance rather than as a weapon. However, those noble warriors who rode in a chariot probably did not fight on foot but mounted their horses and fought with their usual retinue of horsemen. The chariot therefore was used only for a spectacular arrival on the battlefield and was driven away when fighting commenced.

That Celtic chariots ever possessed scythes attached to their wheels seems a myth suggested by the addition of these blades to the hubs and yokes of Persian and Syrian chariots. No archaeological evidence has been discovered of scythed wheels. Although, curiously, an early medieval Irish epic tale, featuring the hero Cuchullain, does refer to a war chariot with 'iron sickles, thin blades, hooks and hard spikes. Its stinging nails fastened to the poles and thongs and bows and lines of the chariot, lacerating heads and bones and bodies.' Most Latin references to Celtic chariots mention them only as a speciality of the Britons, but the remains of chariots have been found in Celtic tombs throughout Europe.

Light, elegant two-wheeled chariots, like those that impressed Caesar, developed from heavier, four-wheeled carts found in Celtic tombs dating from before the fifth century BC. The later two-wheeled vehicles were expertly made. Their spoken wooden wheels were bound with iron tyres. The hubs were also bound with iron bands while the wheels were held on the axle by iron linch-pins. The platform was of wood, usually with curved wood or wicker sides. Two horses pulled the chariot, linked by a yoke to a wooden pole. To these basics were added splendidly crafted rein-rings, flexible bridle-bits, and harness fittings, many decorated with red, yellow and blue enamel. The best contemporary illustrations of Celtic chariots occur on Celtic coins. In the British Museum a chariot is depicted on a tiny bronze coin of the Remi tribe in northern France of the first century BC.

Such images were usually based on the chariots appearing on the reverse of Greek coins, the model for most Gallic coinage. But, in this case, the Celtic craftsman has chosen not to reproduce slavishly the realism of Greek art, but to reduce the chariot to its most vital elements. The horses are portrayed as a series of dynamic balls: muscular thighs, flaring nostrils, and plaited mane. The chariot is represented by one wheel and its semi-circular side, while the driver has been abstracted to arms holding a whip, a head, and three curved rays springing from his back, that is, his cloak flying in the wind.

The evolution of Celtic cavalry and chariotry suggests an origin for this culture in the plains of eastern Europe and Russia, the traditional home of chariot burials and excellent horsemanship. Like all Indo-European speaking people, the Celts were originally from the Eurasian steppes. That the Celts did not lose their talent for riding over their centuries of settlement in central Europe is no doubt due to their close contact with the Cimmerian and Scythian tribes that dominated eastern Europe. It is interesting to note, however, that as with the eastern German tribes of later centuries, the Celts did not adopt the deadly horse-archery characteristic of the steppe tribes. Perhaps they, like the Germans, considered it unmanly for a noble horse-warrior to kill an enemy from afar. Celtic mastery of the horse in battle is a

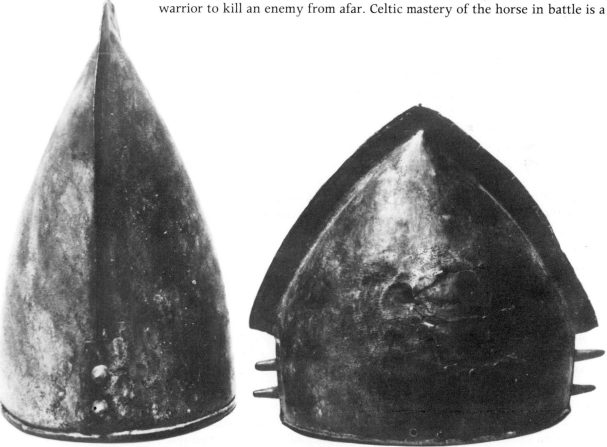

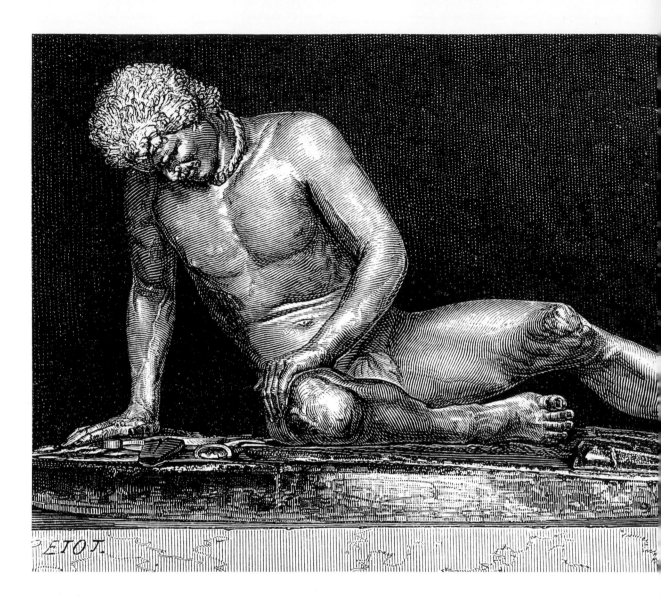

potent thread throughout the history of Celtic warfare, from antiquity to sixteenth-century Ireland. It was this horsemanship that gave the Celts the military power to establish themselves so firmly in European civilization.

For a further fifty years after that raid on Greece, Celtic warriors held absolute control over central Europe, France, Spain and Britain. It was a golden age for the Celts in which their civilization clearly rivalled that of the Greeks and Romans. But then it started to go wrong. Gradually, an ever more confident, ever more united and ambitious Roman Republic made inroads into Celtic territory. The first region to be lost was northern Italy. By 200 BC, after a fierce campaign, virtually all the Italian Celtic tribes had submitted. The Roman war-machine had not only proved superior, but the Romans had even beaten the Celts at their own game. Challenged to single

20

The Dying Gaul, a Roman copy of one of a series of sculptures commissioned by king Attalus I of Pergamum to celebrate his victory over the Celtic Galatians around 230 BC. Reproduced ever since, it has become a symbol of Celtic defeat. This version is an engraving from Duruy's *History of Rome*, 1883.

combat by the chieftain of the Insubres, M. Claudius Marcellus accepted. In the killing ground between the assembled armies, the Roman general rode forward with his shield, spear and sword. Virdomarus, the north Italian Celtic leader, bellowed that he had been born from the waters of the Rhine and would make quick work of the Roman usurper. He dashed in front of his warriors, hurling his spear. But both their spears missed and the chieftains clashed. As each side cheered his leader on, the duel came to a sudden end. A Roman sword slit the Celtic throat and his bent golden torque fell to the ground.

The next Celtic realm to lost control of its own destiny was Spain. Here, many powers converged. Celtic tribesmen had been established in Spain by the fifth century BC. They could not overwhelm the whole native population of this vast country but appear to have made themselves a ruling class over the Iberians in northern and western Spain. Over the years their cultures fused, and ancient historians generally refer to these people as Celtiberians. Along the Mediterranean coast, rivalry between Rome and Carthage over the Spanish ports exploded in war. By the start of the Second Punic War, the Carthaginians controlled most of Spain bar the north-west and Celtiberian mercenaries provided some of their fiercest warriors. However, there were other Celtiberians who resented Carthaginian exploitation of their land and welcomed the intervention of the Romans in Spain. They fought together to rid the land of the Punic invaders. It was an alliance the Celts would regret.

Although their triumphs in the Punic Wars left the Romans with unparalleled power in the Mediterranean, it also left them with many problems. The Celts of northern Italy, ignored during Hannibal's invasion, now rebelled. It took ten years to reconquer them. In Spain, the Celtiberians retained their independence and would not enter into any contract of obedience with the victorious Romans. They had not seen the back of one master merely to submit to another. If the Romans wanted the whole of Spain, they would have to conquer it by arms and not diplomacy. 'This war between the Romans and Celtiberians is called the fiery war,' wrote the contemporary historian Polybius, 'for while wars in Greece or Asia are settled with one or two pitched battles, the battles there dragged on, only brought to a temporary end by the darkness of night. Both sides refused to let their courage flag or their bodies tire.'

The war in Spain was a succession of vicious, indecisive campaigns enduring through most of the second century BC. Roman military incompetence and cruelty was particularly marked and provoked controversy among the politicians in Rome. At the siege of the Celtiberian hill-fort at Pallantia in 136, a Roman commander allowed his supplies to run out. He evacuated his position at night, but, in the hurry, wounded and sick soldiers were left behind. Retreat turned into rout when the Pallantines emerged from their fortress and chased the Romans relentlessly. This general, like many others during the wars, was recalled and deprived of his

21

command. Failure encouraged desperate savagery. Titus Didius set about his suppression of Celtiberian independence with ruthless efficiency. One tribe claimed it had been reduced to banditry because of poverty caused by the war. Didius offered them the lands of a neighbouring Celtic settlement. They agreed, having received similar booty when fighting for the Romans against the Lusitanians. They were invited to the Roman camp where Didius would apportion the land. Once disarmed and inside the stockade, Didius secured the gates and sent in his soldiers to massacre the assembled Celtic men and their families. 'For this,' remarked a disgusted and astonished Roman historian, Appian, 'Didius was actually honoured with a triumph.' Such massacres were matched by numerous military disasters and both served only to stiffen the resistance of the Celtiberians.

'They are no better than bandits,' grumbled the Roman general Scipio Africanus, frustrated yet again by their deception and treachery. 'They may be brave when devastating neighbouring fields, burning villages, and rustling cattle, but are worth nothing in a regular army. They fight with greater confidence in flight than in their weapons.' In truth, the Celtiberians were supreme guerilla warriors. Masters of their own hilly, forested landscape, they exhausted their enemies with relentless skirmishing and raids. Never hanging around long enough for a major confrontation, they humbled the reputation of many Roman generals. After half a century of indecisive conflict, few Roman officers could be found to fill the vacant command posts in Spain. It was a make or break war. But in 134, Publius Cornelius Scipio, the grandson of Scipio Africanus, rose to the challenge. When he arrived in Spain as overall commander, he found a Roman army profoundly demoralized. Discipline was non-existent. Prostitutes and traders, along with fortune-tellers, had to be expelled from the army camps. The soldiers had been reduced to astrology for any signs of a victory. While Scipio retrained his warriors, he surveyed the territory of the Celtiberians. He observed that the town of Numantia in northern, central Spain was a key position and resolved to crush it.

Numantia was a formidable Celtic hill-fort. Set high on a mountain ridge, it was surrounded by dense forest and two fast-flowing rivers cutting through deep ravines. Behind its massive earthen ditches and ramparts, its wood and stone stockade, lay a town with paved streets, blocks of houses, and 8,000 warriors. It had withstood many sieges. In 153, the Romans had employed elephants in their assault. The animals had certainly frightened the Celtic warriors and their horses back into the town, but once the elephants approached the walls the defenders dropped rocks on them. A rock crashed onto the head of one elephant, driving him mad with fury. The great beast let out a terrible scream and turned round, trampling and gouging his own side. The rest of the elephants panicked and soon the Roman army was in tatters as the raging beasts were joined by the Numantines.

Scipio knew well the reputation of Numantia and confined his opening

Brennus receives tribute from the Romans in 390 BC. At the height of their continental power, Celtic warriors shattered a Roman army at Allia and then sacked Rome. Legend has it that when the Romans complained of the weights used by the Celts to measure their tribute gold, the Celtic chieftain Brennus threw his sword onto the scales with the words 'woe to the conquered'.

manoeuvres to plundering the surrounding countryside. His troops harvested the fields, stored what was of immediate use and then burnt everything else. Their activities did not go unheeded and they were constantly ambushed. With losses mounting Scipio decided it was time to deal directly with Numantia. But, rather than attempting to scale its awesome natural and man-made defences, he erected seven forts around the town and linked them with a ditch and palisade. As the Romans laboured, they were joined by neighbouring Celtiberian tribesmen who valued their independence less than the destruction of a powerful rival. Scipio expected the Numantines to disrupt his siege preparations and organised special task forces. If a section of the earthworks was attacked, a red flag should be raised or a fire lit at night so reinforcements could come to their aid. When this first ring was completed another ditch was dug and a palisade built behind it upon an earthern mound eight feet wide and ten feet high. The Numantines, however, still managed to receive provisions from the river Duero. Scipio responded by building a tower each side of the river. To the towers he attached by rope heavy logs studded with knives and spearheads. The tree-trunks bobbed up and down in the furious mountain stream and prevented anyone sailing past. With ballistae and catapults mounted on the towers of his walls, Scipio now waited for starvation to do the rest.

Restless and frustrated, the Numantines led several forays against their besiegers. Emerging out of the night, they clambered over the palisades. They fought with spears and knives, but, above all, they wielded the *falcata*, a heavy cleaver-like cutlass used throughout Spain. According to Livy, the *falcata* could 'cut off arms at the shoulder and sever heads with one chop.' Carthaginian and Greek influences were strong amongst the Celtiberians and it seems likely that, in addition to simple shirts of mail, professional warriors may also have worn horsehair crested helmets and breastplates of strips or scales of metal and leather. They used massive oblong shields and small bucklers, and sometimes a round, concave shield called a *caetra*. In their night attacks, the Numantines probably also used javelins whose three-foot iron blades were tied with rags soaked in pitch. The rags were ignited and the spear flung at an enemy's shield.

These sorties proved unable to break the Roman ring and Rhetogenes, one of the leading Numantine warriors, decided to ride out for help. One cloudy night, with a few comrades and servants, he crossed the no-man's-land between the two earthworks. Carrying a folding scaling-ladder, the Celts scrambled up the first wall and silenced the guards. They then hauled up their horses and dashed along the palisade to freedom. They rode off to the hill-fort of the Arevaci, entreating them as blood relations to come to their aid. The Arevaci feared the retaliation of the Romans and refused. Rhetogenes rode onto a town called Lutia. There, the young men sympathised with the Numantines and prepared to join them. But older citizens doubted the wisdom of this and informed the Romans. Scipio reacted immediately. He surrounded Lutia the next day and demanded to see the

Model of a reconstructed Celtic chariot. Such chariots were mainly used for the spectacular arrival of chief warriors on the battlefield: intended to overawe the enemy.

young warriors. Under threat of attack, the young Celts emerged from the town. Scipio seized the 400 and had their hands cut off. That night he was back at Numantia.

As the weeks passed, hunger made the Numantines consider a negotiated surrender. Avarus, their leader, approached Scipio with terms of settlement. But Scipio was not interested. He would accept only absolute capitulation. The Numantines were furious and murdered Avarus and his envoys, thinking they may have made private terms for themselves with the Romans. Within the town, the situation became desperate. With no food at all, some citizens resorted to cannibalism. Finally, famine and disease broke their spirit. They surrendered, but many took their own lives. Appian, the Roman chronicler of these events, was moved by the valiant endurance of the Numantines. He wondered at how 8,000 Celtiberians could only be brought to heel by 60,000 Romans; and not even in a pitched battle, but through the prolonged agony of a siege. The survivors of the conflict were a strange and pathetic sight. 'Their bodies were foul, their hair and nails long, and they were smeared with dirt,' wrote Appian. 'In their eyes there was a fearful expression: an expression of anger, pain, weariness, and the awareness of having eaten human flesh.' Scipio was untouched by the spectacle. Having chosen fifty warriors for his triumph, he sold the rest of the Numantines into slavery and set fire to their town. Their territory was divided among neighbouring tribes, ensuring bitter feuds for years to come. The heartland of Celtiberian resistance had been devastated and 133 BC is generally accepted as the end of the Spanish war.

There were many rebellions, but essentially Celtiberian independence had been smothered by the Roman Empire. That said, there was no extensive Roman colonisation of Spain. Only a few legionary veterans settled around the prosperous coastal towns. Most of the Spanish interior remained under the direct control of Celtiberian warlords, even though they now did homage to Rome. Their culture continued strong, as did their warriors. At the end of the second century BC, when the wandering Germanic tribesmen of the Cimbri turned away from Italy and rode into Spain, it was Celtiberian warbands who confronted them. The Cimbri, allied with the Teutones, had already devastated three Roman armies. In Spain they met warriors of their own kind and after two years of raiding, their rough reception form the Celtiberians forced them back upon Italy. United again with the Teutones, who had received a similarly tough time from the Celts of northern France, they advanced to defeat at the hands of a reformed Roman army in 102.

It has been suggested that the Cimbri and Teutones were not Germans but Celts. Many ancient historians saw little difference between the two barbarian peoples and it is more than likely that this horde consisted of many Celtic freebooters from France and central Europe. Certainly, the plundering movements of these tribes were typical of the intertribal warfare that wracked non-Roman Europe. The immediate effect of these raiders in southern Europe was to stir up other Celtic tribes against the Romans. Only a decade earlier, the lands of Mediterranean Gaul had been annexed by the Romans. Now these tribesmen rebelled. In the Balkans, the Germans had been prevented from advancing any further by the Scordisci of Yugoslavia. Once they rolled back the Teutones, these tribesmen took advantage of Roman weakness and invaded their territory in Greece. Emboldened by their strength against the Cimbri, the Celtiberians again threw off Roman Imperialism. Eventually, after a disastrous start, the Romans took control of the situation, but it was a profound crisis that reminded them of the force of the Celts.

Realising that a successful military career was the best way to political power, the young Julius Caesar placed himself in the forefront of the border wars with the Celts. His first military experience was won against the Celtiberians. He then placed himself in command of the provinces of Cisalpine Gaul (northern Italy) and Provence. The ambition of this one man was to bring the Celtic warlords of France to their knees. But conquests are not won by brilliant leaders alone. As Caesar himself admitted: 'Fortune, which has great influence on affairs generally and especially in war, produces by a slight disturbance of balance important changes in human affairs.' In Gaul, the Roman's good fortune was to be the same that had dogged the independence of the Celtiberian chieftains. In this case, the threat of the Carthaginians was replaced by a German invasion of Gaul, but, as before, those Celtic chieftains who applied to the Romans for help were to find that they had played into the hands of a more ruthless master.

From 65 to 60 BC, a confederation of German tribes known as the Suebi were led by a dynamic warlord called Ariovistus. Recognising his power, Gallic chieftains employed the Suebi to defeat their Celtic rivals, but Ariovistus demanded in payment the land of his allies. Soon, Celtic warlords were asking the Romans to intervene against the German invaders. But the Senate did not like to back losers, entering into friendly relations with Ariovistus. One of the principal architects of this agreement was Caesar. The disarray of the Celtic tribes encouraged Caesar to move his legions westwards from Aquileia to the Rhone. He had planned to build a reputation for himself against the Dacians, but the inter-tribal conflict of the Gauls and their fear of the Germans seemed a golden opportunity. Events came to a head when the Helvetii of Switzerland wished to move out of the

Reverse of a British coin showing a horse and wheel of a chariot. Many Celtic coins were based on Greek or Roman prototypes, but on this one Celtic craftsmanship predominates and the chariot has been abstracted to its powerful essentials. Found in the south of England near Silchester, now in the British Museum, London.

Iron Celtiberian falcata, fourth to first century BC, now in the National Archaelogical Museum, Madrid. The iron scabbard frames of this sword remain to show how it was usually carried in a leather sheath hung from a baldric.

way of the Suebi and cross through the neighbouring Celtic territory of the
Aedui to western France. The Aedui asked Caesar for assistance. With an
army of Roman legionaries and Gallic cavalry he complied. The Helvetii
gave him a tough time, using their wagon laager as a strong defensive
position, but eventually they were subdued. Caesar massacred 6,000 of
them and sent the rest back to Switzerland. Such ruthless strength clearly
impressed the Celts and they redoubled their requests for his help against
Ariovistus.

These facts we know from Caesar's own chronicle of the events. In his
account he emphasises the Gallic fear of the Germans, their disunity, and
their desperate plea for Roman assistance. The Celts are portrayed as a once
mighty nation, now less brave than the Germans and in need of outside
warriors to fight their battles. Such a view, of course, makes Caesar appear
as the protector of the Gauls, whose entry into their territory is not an
invasion, but in response to their repeated invitations. This begs cynicism.
Celtic tribes had been determined and daring enough to defeat both Roman
and Teutonic armies only fifty years earlier. And yet this is an eye-witness
account: why should Caesar write of the Gauls with barely disguised
contempt when it is in his own interest to make them seem a mighty, bold
people, so as to make his own victory over them even greater? This he does
do, but later in his account when describing their noble last-stand at Alesia.
Caesar has his cake and eats it. In the meantime, Caesar reneged on Rome's
friendship with Ariovistus and threw the Germans back across the Rhine.
He now exploited his strong position in Gaul and annexed the land of the
Aedui and the Sequani. Their weakness and supposed invitation is his
excuse.

The Belgic tribes of northern France saw the error of their Celtic kinsmen
and combined to confront Caesar's legions. The Belgae were a notoriously

Iberian dagger found near Cordoba, now in the National Archaelogical Museum, Madrid. The blade is 8 cm broad at the base and 19 cm ($7\frac{1}{2}$ in) long.

fierce confederation, hardened by years of border conflict with the Germans. They were part German themselves. On receiving this news, Caesar raised two more legions to add to his six already quartered in Gaul, and rapidly advanced on Belgic territory. His speed surprised the Remi, the nearest of the Belgic tribes, and they immediately caved in, offering him hostages and military intelligence. Caesar dispatched his Aeduan auxiliaries to plunder Belgic land, while he sat tight. The ferocious reputation of the Belgae discouraged Caesar from meeting them in a pitched battle, so he tested their stamina with numerous cavalry skirmishes. The main Roman army remained in a camp protected by marshes and entrenchments. The Belgae tried to entice the Romans into a full-scale confrontation, but Caesar's Gallic horsemen continued to keep them at a distance. As the skirmishing endured, the supplies of the Belgae began to run out. Like most barbarian armies, it appears they did not organise a proper supply train, so unless they gained sufficient food from their plundering their campaigns lacked staying power. When reports of Aeduan raids on their own territory added to their frustration, the Belgic horde retreated with the Gallo-Roman horsemen in hot pursuit. Thus the Belgic confederation was reduced tribe by tribe by a Romano-Gallic force in which the Celtic auxiliaries of Caesar played a vital part. Without doubt, the Celts could be their own worst enemy. And yet, to impose such concepts of a national identity on all Celts is misplaced, for the Belgae were as different and alien to the Celtic tribes to the south of them as they were to the Romans, even though they spoke a similar language. A shared culture never stopped the Romans or Greeks from ripping themselves to pieces.

A Gallic horseman proudly drawn by Alphonse de Neuville on the eve of the Franco-Prussian War. From Guizot's 1870 L'Histoire de France, it reflects a nationalistic pride in the Celtic roots of French culture.

Throughout the campaigns in Gaul, Diviciacus, chieftain of the Aedui, was constantly at Caesar's side, urging his Celtic confederates to submit peacefully to Roman domination. As the Roman war-machine rolled on, more and more Gallic warriors joined its legions. So far, in his march through Gaul, Caesar had had good excuses for his agression: the invitations of the Aedui, the attacks of the Belgae. But in 57 BC he sent a detachment under the command of a subordinate to the lands of the Atlantic coast. Their subsequent reduction of this peaceful area was unprovoked and patently revealed Caesar's intention to conquer the whole of Gaul. The next year, recovering from the shock of Roman occupation, the Celts of Brittany, led by the Veneti, took up arms. The Veneti were a maritime power, deriving much wealth from their shipping of British tin from Cornwall to Gallic traders. Their strongholds stood on headlands or islands in tidal estuaries which were cut off from the land for most of the time by the sea.

As the Romans approached the Atlantic coast, the Veneti strengthened their fleet and gathered fellow tribesmen, including many warriors from Britain. Caesar was secure in his excuse this time: the quelling of a tribe who had already submitted and the punishment of a terrorist kidnapping of Roman envoys. He again employed the assistance of friendly Celts who supplied him with Gallic ships built along the Loire. With his land forces he tried to capture the Breton strongholds. Using all the ingenuity of Roman siegecraft, he had huge dykes constructed to the island fortresses. But no sooner had these been completed than the defenders simply evacuated into awaiting ships and moved to another fortress. The lack of natural harbours and the rough ocean weather made Roman assaults by sea difficult. The considerable advantage of knowing the local seaways lay very much with the Veneti. But, as elsewhere, there was no shortage of Celts ready to assist the Romans.

Local Gauls presented the Romans with a rapidly-built fleet which cannot have been very different from that of the Veneti. 'They have flat bottoms.' wrote Caesar of the Gallic ships, 'which enables them to sail in shallow coastal water. Their high bows and sterns protect them from heavy seas and violent storms, as do their strong hulls made entirely from oak. The cross-timbers—beams a foot wide—are secured with iron nails as thick as a man's thumb. Their anchors are secured with chains not ropes, while their sails are made of raw hide or thin leather, so as to stand up to the violent Atlantic winds.'

When Caesar's fleet was ready, he confronted the Veneti in the Loire estuary. As the boats crashed into each other, legionaries and their Gallic allies watched the battle from the cliff-tops. The Romans in the boats—all land soldiers—were at a loss as to how to tackle the Gallic seamen. They improvised with scythes attached to long poles and used them to cut the Celtic rigging. With their sails fluttering uselessly and apparently no oars to assist them, the Celtic ships soon lost control. Several Roman boats then locked onto individual Celtic ships and boarded them. The Celtic sailors were overwhelmed by the armoured Romans and the fleet of the Veneti broke up. A fall in the wind prevented many from escaping and the majority of the Gallic force was captured. This seems a particularly miserable defeat for the Celts. A fleet of expert seamen shattered by landlubber Romans making do with scythes. Caesar's account doesn't ring true. It seems more likely that the fighting on the Roman side was conducted wholly by Gallic auxiliaries used to sailing. Whatever the actual details, this defeat of 56 BC was a crushing one for the Atlantic Gauls. Caesar had many of his prisoners executed and the rest sold as slaves to his legionaries and allied Celtic tribes.

Over the next couple of years, Caesar suppressed local rebellions in northern Gaul. An expedition was made to Britain on the pretext of quelling those tribes who had assisted the Veneti. At this time, south-east England had been overrun by Belgic immigrants. Their warlord Cassivellaunus was gradually extending his control over the native Celts. Again, it seemed as if Celtic dissension might aid Caesar, but on this occasion the Celts put up a stiff guerilla resistance and Britain remained an independent Celtic realm. Throughout his campaigns so far, Caesar had restricted himself to securing a ring of conquests around central Gaul without venturing into the interior. But as he consolidated this position, perhaps preparing for that next stage of his conquest, the Celts sprang out at Caesar with a vengeance.

Bronze anthropoid hilt of an iron sword from Salon in France, around the second century BC, now in the British Museum, London.

The Celtic warriors were led by an Arvernian chieftain called Vercingetorix. A powerful personality, he instilled a strict discipline into his warrior retinue. Neighbouring tribes were asked to submit hostages to him and disaffection was punished with death. No waverers would be tolerated. Equally determined, Caesar plunged straight into the heartland of the Arverni. Initially successful, he was savaged by the Gauls at the hill-fort of Gergovia. At one stage, the Romans were surprised by the arrival of their own Gallic cavalry, for these auxiliaries were clad identically to other Celtic horsemen. According to Caesar, friendly troops usually 'left their right shoulders uncovered as an agreed sign.' With this defeat, Caesar's aura of invincibility was broken and Celtic tribes throughout Gaul joined the independence fighters. Even the Aedui threw in their lot with Vercingetorix. Caesar was shaken. He had to reinforce his cavalry with German horsemen.

The final confrontation was enacted at the siege of Alesia in 52 BC. It may have been that Vercingetorix hoped to hold Caesar outside the hill-fort until Gallic reinforcements arrived to crush the Romans between both forces. But Caesar employed Roman siegecraft to good effect and protected his rear with a second chain of earthworks. When the massive relief army arrived, the Roman force was strained to its limits but eventually fought them off. Alesia was then starved into surrender. With the capture of Vercingetorix, Gallic independence broke up and was eventually snuffed out. An overall peace was made and Caesar withdrew the majority of his troops from Gaul. Not only was the siege of Alesia the last major battle of the Gallic wars, it

symbolized the extinction of Celtic liberty in Europe. Rebellions would come and go, but never again would a warlord independent of Rome rule a continental Celtic realm. Celtic independence remained only in Britain and Ireland.

This then is the story of Celtic defeat in Europe, an account based on the legends of Greece and Rome. For the chronicles describing these events are frequently the work of Romans and Greeks writing hundreds of years after the action they recount. Pausanias compiled his account of the Celtic invasion of Greece, the fullest we have, almost 500 years afterwards. It may have been based on earlier records but essentially it is a classical view of the Celts as inferior barbarians cowed by the civilization of Greece. Appian is a more realistic historian, cynical of his Empire's disgraceful conduct in Spain, but still his accounts of the Celtiberians are 400 years later and laced with hackneyed descriptions of noble but vanquished Celts. Caesar's memoirs are, of course, based on eye-witness experience but a calculating bias ensures that the inherent weakness of the Gauls is emphasised to excuse Roman intervention. This is the Mediterranean myth of the Celts. From now on, as Britain fights to maintain itself as the last Celtic bastion, we begin to see the struggle of the Celts through their own culture, through their own legends.

The Battle for Britain

Cuchulainn—ancient Irish warlord, Hound of Ulster—slept for three days. The men of Connacht had pushed a cattle raid deep into his territory. Short of warriors, he had had to restrain himself to brief, surprise attacks on the plunderers. Many of the enemy had been killed, but he was wounded and exhausted. In the delirium of his pain and fatigue, a heavenly phantom advised him to rest. After three days, Cuchulainn awoke. An excitement possessed him. Blood quickly pulsed through his body and his face turned red. He felt good. He felt fit for a feast, fit for fighting. He instructed a retainer to prepare his chariot.

The charioteer donned a tunic of supple stitched deers' leather. He wore an iron battle-cap and daubed a circle of yellow on his forehead to distinguish him from his master. Over his two horses he secured a harness studded with iron plates, spikes and barbs. Every surface of the chariot bristled with blades. Every inch had a ripping hook or a tearing nail. Finally the driver cast a protecting spell over the chariot and grabbed his iron-shod goad.

With the chariot ready, Cuchulainn prepared himself for battle. His followers strapped on his armour. A tunic of waxed skin plates, several layers thick, was tied securely with rope so it would not burst at the onset of his fighting rage. Over this, the warlord wore a thick, wide battle-belt of tanned leather from the choicest hides of his prize cattle. This covered him from his waist to his armpits. Around his stomach was a silk apron embroidered with gold, over which a battle apron of the darkest leather was

Roman horseman riding over northern British warriors. Detail of a second-century dedication slab from the eastern end of the Antonine Wall where it meets the Firth of Forth.

strapped. On his head was placed a crested helmet. Within the iron, his long battle cry echoed so as to cause the demons of the air and glen to scream back. Cuchulainn now reached for his weapons: an ivory hilted sword, several short swords, throwing and stabbing spears, a five-pronged trident, and a dark red curved shield. He held a shield stout enough to keep a wild boar in its hollow, with a rim so razor sharp that it could cut a single hair— a shield as deadly as his spear or sword.

Loaded and reinforced with all his battle gear, Cuchulainn began to work himself up into a fighting fury. A spasm tore through his body. It distorted him, made him a monstrous thing. Every bone and organ shook like a tree in a storm. His insides made a twist within his skin. His shins filled with the

37

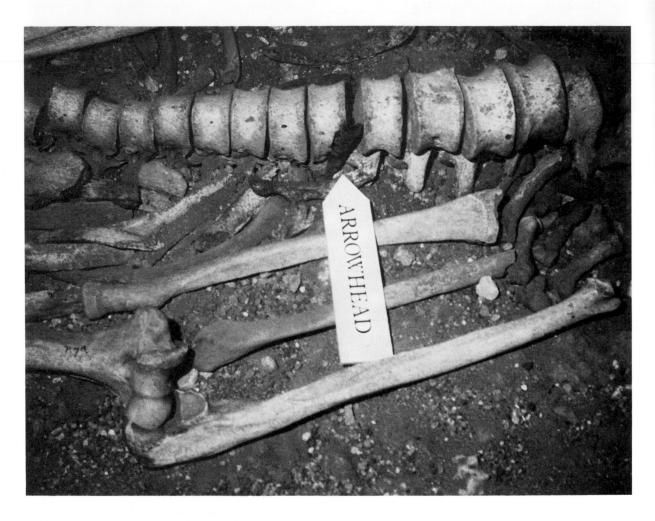

ARROWHEAD

bulging muscles of his calves. Balls of sinew as big as a warrior's fist pumped up his body. His head swelled and throbbed. Veins dilated. Suddenly, he gulped one eye deep into his head so not even a wild crane could pull it out from his skull. The skin of his cheeks then peeled back from his jaws to reveal the gristle and bone of his gullet. His jaws crashed together and foam oozed up out of his throat. His hair twisted and bristled like a red thornbush. Dazzling lights and thick black smoke rose above his head. A broad halo emerged over his brow. With the transformation completed, Cuchulainn leaped onto his chariot. He had no fear. He was a mad man. A hero.

Cuchulainn burst upon his enemies like a thunder storm. His chariot wheeled furiously in the mud: its iron tyres dug up earth tracks high enough for a fortress rampart. At the end of the day, the warlord had slain hundreds of his enemies. Nothing was too great or too insignificant to be spared Cuchulainn's blades. Chieftains and warriors, horses and dogs, women and children. All were slaughtered.

Roman ballista bolt-head lodged in the spine of a Celtic warrior. A victim of the assault on Maiden Castle by Vespasian in AD 43, his bones now lie in the Dorset County Museum, Dorchester.

The next morning, Cuchulainn arose to display himself to his followers. He paraded in front of his women and poets, reassuring them that his hideous battle form was now replaced by a handsome image, a youthful man whose hair was brown at its roots, rising through blood-red to a golden yellow at its tips. This hair fell luxuriantly in three coils over his shoulders. Around him was wrapped a purple cloak secured with a brooch of light gold and silver. Beneath he wore a fretted silk tunic and a warrior's apron of deep red royal silk. To his back was attached a gold-rimmed shield with five discs on a crimson background. From his belt hung a sword with a guard of ivory and gold. In his hands, he gripped nineteen human heads and shook them at his followers. All his people crowded forward to marvel at the hero.

This account of the Ulster warlord Cuchulainn comes from the *Tain Bo Cuailnge*: The Cattle Raid on Cuailnge. An Irish epic tale dated to the eighth century AD, it is believed to be centuries older, perhaps even pre-Christian. It is a terrifying vision of the ritual and glamour of violence. To his followers, this savage executioner is a hero of supernatural stature. For him, psychopathic aggression is physical strength. The epic tale is our deepest insight to the psychology of Celtic warriors: the importance of display and parade; the working up into a fighting rage. The belief in a hero's halo was widespread throughout the Celtic world and sometimes even exploited by non-Celtic adversaries. According to L. Annaeus Florus, around 130 AD, a Roman centurion struck terror into the Moesi by carrying a flaming brazier on his helmet. Other supernatural qualities ascribed to Celtic warriors in battle are elaborated in the Tain. Cuchulainn repeatedly leaps high in the air to come down heavily on his opponent's shield. Strange weapons are referred to, such as the legendary *gae bolga*, 'the lightning spear': a javelin that enters the body as one blade, but then bursts open into thirty barbs. Only by cutting away chunks of flesh could it be removed. The Tain also demonstrates that though there might be a sense of respect, even fair play, between two renowned warriors meeting in single combat, all other living things in a battle zone were vulnerable to brutal slaughter.

That such an epic tale as the Tain could be woven out of a relatively minor cattle raid should not be surprising. This is the stuff of Celtic warfare. Major campaigns against foreign enemies involving armies of united tribes—thousands of warriors strong—were rare. Most conflict was centred around the pursuit and prevention of plundering expeditions by a martial elite of warlords and their retainers, separate from the great body of tribesmen. However, to look upon the Tain as a war fought over the mere material gain of a few prize cattle is to miss the point. The rustling of cattle from an opponent's territory was simply an excuse to test that rival's strength. If a warlord allowed such a challenge to his authority without retaliation, he risked losing the respect of his own warriors as well as that of outsiders. This revelation of weakness could encourage an outsider to embark on a full-scale campaign in the belief that the victim was vulnerable. It might even encourage a coup d'état within the clan as a more

able warlord arose to avenge the insult to his people. For Celtic warlords—
as with all men of authority—a lack of respect means an actual lack of
power. A cattle raid, therefore, had to be met with forceful retribution,
otherwise worse could follow.

This endemic intertribal combat may have produced a hardened, highly
experienced class of professional fighters but it also lay Celtic realms open
to determined, strategically-wise foreigners. In 43 AD, the Atrebates of
southern Britain fell back before the dominant Catuvellauni. The chieftain
of the Atrebates asked the Romans for help and the Roman invasion began.
Roman conquests in Britain were aided by further tribal dissension as well
as friendly Celtic auxiliaries hoping for favours in the new regime. In just
over fifty years, all England and most of Wales and Scotland had been
absorbed into the Latin Empire. It is little wonder then that Gildas, a
northern Briton, complained around 540 AD that 'It has always been true of
this people that we are weak in beating off the weapons of the outside
enemy but strong in fighting amongst each other.'

The plight of the Celts under Roman rule was not one of only abject
slavery or bold revolts. More often than not, in the Roman provinces of
Spain, France and Britain, Celtic chieftains continued to rule over their
tribes and territory. These warlords might have Latin names, live in Roman
villas, and fight alongside legionary armies, but they were still Celts. In a
curious way, Roman Imperialism did not totally destroy Celtic power. It
may even have strengthened it. Celtic warlords accepted the material
luxuries, military sophistication, Christian religion and Latin literature of the
Romans, but they still remained in control of their own land. Indeed, the
military back-up of the Romans enabled them to keep their land free of
Germanic raiders. Celtic chieftains would have to make tribute to their
Imperial overlords, but essentially it was they who were there in the field to
defend their own territory against all marauders. They maintained the
Roman way of life because they liked it. But, beneath it all, it was Celtic
tribal loyalties and customs that kept the ordinary man in order, not Roman
citizenship. Thus, the Roman Empire in western Europe can be seen not so
much as a defeated Celtic people under the yoke of Roman Imperialism, but
a confederation of tribes held together by Romanized Celtic warlords
paying feudal homage to a supreme, but absentee landlord.

This state of affairs became obvious when the agents of the Emperor,
with their mercenary retinues, cleared out of Britain at the beginning of the
fifth century to concentrate on the defence of Italy. Britain did not
suddenly revert to a purely Celtic realm, naked without its Roman
defenders. Of course, the warlords of Britain could always do with
continental reinforcements, but they could also see to their own defence.
For centuries they had dealt with Irish and German pirates and the
plundering of the Picts. This was nothing new, but typical of old scores yet
to be settled. Around the hard core of their retainers, the British warlords
did as the Romans did. They supplemented their forces with mercenary

Northern ramparts and ditches of Maiden Castle, an Iron Age hillfort of the first century BC, near Dorchester, south-west Britain. The massive earth ramparts were originally surmounted by a wood palisade.

recruits from the coastal tribes of Germany. In the early years of the fifth century, it was Vortigern—overlord of the Romano-Celts in south-eastern England—who invited three shiploads of Saxons to assist him. Just like other provincial governors of Roman Europe, he settled these warriors along his borders as a buffer against raiders.

The Celts relished their inheritance of *romanitas*. In future centuries, they wrote about the Roman Empire as a time of greatness. In the Welsh saga of the *Mabinogion*—a fourteenth-century manuscript whose stories are much older—a Roman warlord Magnus Maximus is idealised. 'The ruler Maxen was Emperor of Rome,' it recalls, 'and he was handsomer and wiser and better suited to be an Emperor than any of his predecessors.' A senior officer in the Romano-Celtic army of Britain—probably stationed at Caerleon in South Wales—Magnus was a Spaniard, perhaps a Celtiberian. It may even have been the dream of establishing a truly Romano-Celtic Empire that excited his ambition. Whatever the spur, he was acclaimed Emperor by his followers in 383 AD. Leading a Romano-Celtic band of adventurers across

41

the Channel, he defeated the Emperor Gratian in Gaul and proclaimed himself lord of all the ancient Celtic realms of Britain, France and Spain. He had a precedent: a century earlier the Roman general Postumus had similarly ruled an *imperium Galliarum* for ten years. In events such as this, it is difficult to know whether to see Magnus as a rebel against the Roman Emperor, or simply one of many warlords pushing a little far the flexibility of Romano-Celtic command of western Europe. According to the tale in the *Mabinogion*, it is British warriors who storm the very walls of Rome and give the city to Magnus. Many of these Celtic warriors then settled in Brittany. In truth, Magnus never made it to Rome but was assassinated in Aquileia in 388. In Britain his legend lived on and many Welsh kings claimed him as their forefather.

Magnus was one of several Romano-Celtic warlords who assumed political as well as military control over their territories. Carausis was a Gaul from the coast of Belgium. Because of his profound sea-knowledge, he was given a naval command in the Channel with orders to crush the North Sea pirates. It was the late third century and Saxon raids on Britain and France were increasingly ferocious. From his bases in northern Gaul, Carausis successfully countered the freebooters; almost too successfully, for he was suspected of waiting for the priates to carry out their raids and only then, on their way back, would he pounce and confiscate their treasure for himself. But, before he could be arrested, he sailed to Britain and there proclaimed himself Emperor. Wild seas and the expertise of his Celtic fleet prevented the Romans from any immediate action.

For ten years Carausis prospered and built a string of forts along the coast of eastern England. These were massive fortifications, earthworks and stone walls, and intended as much to repel Roman invaders as Saxon raiders. But the Imperial Caesar Constantius was determined to end this Celtic break-

away state and set about blockading the Gaul's main continental base at Boulogne. While the French base succumbed to siege, Carausis was murdered by one of his retainers and in 296 a final assault brought eastern Britain back under direct Imperial control. During his reign, Carausis had done much to strengthen Britain's naval defences. In the next century, these were further improved by the introduction of camouflaged scouting craft. According to Vegetius, these boats had their sails and rigging dyed blue. With the sailors similarly disguised in blue tunics and painted faces, the craft acted as an early warning system against pirates.

The break-up of the western Roman Empire was not so much a sudden onslaught of Barbarian savages upon the Imperial frontiers as a gradual realisation among Germanic auxiliaries that it was they who wielded real power in the Romano-Celtic provinces. They arose from their frontier military settlements to assume political control. This happened in Britain. The Romano-Celtic overlord Vortigern had many problems. Irish and Pict raiders impinged on British land in Wales and northern England. Within Romano-British ranks, Vortigern contended with Ambrosius for the Emperorship of Britain. Added to this was the fear that Ambrosius might capitalise on continental Catholic fears of heresy in Britain and bring a Romano-Gallic army across the Channel. To strengthen his military position within and without, Vortigern invited Saxon mercenaries into his country and settled them on the island of Thanet in the river Thames. Initially they were welcome and proved useful, but the situation deteriorated.

Bronze helmet crest in the form of a wild boar. Found at Gaer Fawr, Welshpool, Powys, north-east Wales, now in the National Museum of Wales, Cardiff.

43

Hengist, the leading Saxon chieftain, was a shrewd warlord. He exploited Vortigern's weaknesses, his bitter rivalry with Ambrosius and other magnates. 'We are few,' he told the British overlord, 'but if you wish, we can send home for more men to fight for you and your people.' Across the Channel came nineteen more ships packed with Saxon adventurers. As Hengist amassed his warriors, tensions grew between them and the British. The Saxons complained that their monthly payments were inadequate. If they were to continue propping up Vortigern, then he would have to give them more supplies. Vortigern granted them land in Kent, but soon the Saxons were plundering further afield. By the 440s, the Saxons had openly turned against their paymasters and stormed several British towns.

'In this devastation by the pagans,' wrote the Romano-British Gildas, 'there was no burial to be had except in the ruins of houses or the bellies of beasts and birds.' But, as the Saxons consolidated their conquests in Kent and East Anglia, the British gathered their native troops and counter-attacked. Surprised perhaps by the strength of the Britons, the Saxons were shaken in two battles by Vortimer, son of Vortigern. On the banks of the river Darenth and again at Horseford or Aylesford, the Saxons suffered heavy losses. Horsa, one of their chieftains, was killed. In a third battle, according to the British chronicler Nennius, 'in the open country by the Inscribed Stone on the shore of the Gallic Sea, the barbarians were beaten. They fled to their ships and many were drowned as they clambered aboard them like women.' The Saxons fell back on their stronghold at Thanet where they were besieged three times.

Sending for reinforcements from the continent, the Saxons eventually broke out of Thanet and the war against the British ebbed and flowed, with the ordinary peasant Briton suffering most from the plundering of both sides. Upon the death of Vortimer, the Saxons resorted to negotiations to better their position. The ageing Vortigern could not maintain a state of war against the Saxons indefinitely without the political and financial support of all Britain's warlords. This was not forthcoming and old rivalries forced Vortigern to accept Hengist's suggestions of an armistice. The two sides agreed to meet, unarmed, to conclude a treaty. But Hengist ordered his men to hide their daggers in their boots. As the noblemen gathered, the Saxons sprang their trap and slaughtered 300 leading British aristocrats. Vortigern was spared his life on condition he handed over Essex and Sussex to the Germans. With Hengist now riding high, many more German warriors sailed to Britain. Over the next fifty years, Saxons, Angles and Jutes secured their hold over southern and eastern England.

The Anglo-Saxon wars in Britain were part of a broader conflict across north-west Europe. In France, the Romano-Gauls had long protected the coasts of Brittany against Saxon pirates with their river-mouth forts. During the fifth century, the Romano-Gallic warlords were joined by British immigrants. These were the cream of Romano-British aristocracy from Cornwall: some fleeing before Irish raiders, others hoping for closer

Iron spear heads from Llyn Cerrig Bach, Anglesey, north-west Wales, now in the National Museum of Wales, Cardiff.

associations with Imperial Roman culture. Allied sometimes with the Franks, it was this Romano-Gallo-British amalgam—the Bretons—who fought most ferociously against the Saxons of the North Sea and the Goths settled in central France. And then, in later centuries, when the Franks had established themselves as a separate kingdom, it was the Bretons who maintained Brittany as an independent Celtic state against the Merovingian and Carolingian dynasties. In the sixth century, Gregory of Tours records their damaging raids on the cities of Nantes and Rennes. Two hundred years later, the Bretons were still resisting and Charlemagne had to devote an entire campaign to their conquest. Even then this proved fragile and during his reign they were in constant rebellion.

Back in the fifth century, the security of the Bretons depended on the efforts of independent Romano-Gallic warlords like Ecdicius. With only his

'The Free Northern Britons surprising the Roman Wall between the Tyne and the Solway'. An engraving from a drawing by William B. Scott in the *Illustrated London News* of 1843. Chosen by the newspaper from a national competition of cartoons by history painters, it reveals a burgeoning British interest in their Celtic past.

private income to fund him and no assistance from other magnates, Ecdicius gathered together a·small force of horse-warriors. He then set about ambushing the local plundering expeditions of the Goths of central France. So hard did the Gallic horsemen harass the Goth raiders that, according to the account of Sidonius, the bandits had no time to retrieve their dead. Instead, the raiders preferred to cut the heads off their comrades so that at least Ecdicius would not know how many Goths he had slain by the hairstyle of the corpses. When this private band of man-hunters relieved the town of Clermont from Goth bandits, Ecdicius was received rapturously by the townspeople. 'What tears and rejoicing greeted you!' wrote Sidonius, brother-in-law of Ecdicius. 'Some townspeople kissed away the dust that covered you. Others caught hold of your bridle, thick with blood and foam. When you wished to take off your helmet, the clamouring citizens unclasped the bands of iron. Some entangled themselves in the straps of your greaves. Some counted the dents along the edges of your sword blunted by slaughter. While others fingered the holes made by blade and point amid your shirt of mail. You bore all these stupidities of your welcome with good grace.'

These Gallic guerilla actions took place around 471 AD and may well have been inspired by stories of the successful resistance of the Britons led by Ambrosius Aurelianus. Ten years earlier, Ambrosius had commanded a similar task force of horse-warriors against the Saxons. Raised from the Romano-Celtic estates of the West Country and Wales, these swift-moving, professional, largely aristocratic horsemen hammered the Saxons in a series of confrontations. The Celtic warriors called each other *Combrogi*, 'fellow countrymen', a word probably derived from the Latin *cives*. It is the origin of *Cymry* and *Cumbri*, names still used by the Welsh and north-west British to denote their Celtic separateness from the Germanic English. For a hundred years, the British and Saxons fought their border wars. At sometime during the conflict Ambrosius died. He was replaced by an equally competent warlord, a major Romano-British land-owner and expert leader of horsemen: Arthur.

All we truly know about Arthur is a list of twelve battles he fought throughout Britain. Many of these have been traced to sites in northern England and may have been conflicts not with the Germans but against the Celtic warrior tribes of Scotland who were as much of a problem. Arthur probably commanded a flexible force of aristocratic young horse-warriors, riding from Roman fort to Roman fort across Celtic Britain. His stronghold in southern Wales may well have been Caerleon: a stalwart Roman fortress of earthwork ramparts and timber-laced stone walls, long in use after the last foreign Imperial garrison left. Was this Camelot? The British chronicler Nennius states that 'Arthur carried the image of the Holy Mary, the Everlasting Virgin, on his shield,' while the Welsh Annals declare that he wore 'the Cross of Our Lord Jesus Christ across his shoulders.' It seems likely that the Christian Romano-Britons considered their campaign against the pagan Saxons a Crusade and carried out their warfare with an outraged fervour: avenging the sight of their churches burnt and sacked by the Germanic barbarians.

At the end of the fifth century, Arthur's string of victories culminated in the battle of Badon Hill. Nennius describes the hot water that bubbled up at the natural springs of Badon as one of the wonders of Britain. It therefore seems likely that Badon was the Roman settlement of Bath and the battle took place on the hills overlooking its villas, temples, and hot-water bathing complex. It was a city worth fighting for and it was probably the Saxons of Wessex and Sussex who wished to claim it. The general conflict may have been a siege as Gildas describes it, for the Welsh Annals say that the battle lasted three days and three nights. But, in the event, it seems to have been decided by a grand cavalry charge in which Arthur slaughtered many of the enemy. So decisive was this victory that no other major battles are mentioned for two decades. Arthur appears to have successfully blocked the Saxon advance into the West Country.

Germanic desire proved relentless, however, and around 515 the British defence of the West was shattered. In the battle of Camlann, perhaps a siege of Caerleon, Arthur was killed. Nevertheless, Celtic resistance remained persistent enough to deny the Saxons part of the West Country for a further fifty years and most of Wales and Cornwall for centuries. In the wake of Germanic supremacy in Europe, it could be said that this part of Britain was the last independent Romano-Celtic province. But its defenders were not Roman legionaries but Celtic horsemen. It was these Celtic warriors who called the Saxons 'barbari' and preserved Latin culture. This is Arthur's success and the origin of his legend as the supreme Christian knight.

The conversion of the Anglo-Saxons to Christianity at the end of the sixth century brought no immediate softening of hostilities, but provided yet more causes for conflict. Around 603, St Augustine, the first Archbishop of Saxon Canterbury, set about bringing the British of the Celtic Church into line with Catholicism, altering their customs and rites in accordance with the Church of Rome. The Britons referred to their holy men and received the following advice. 'If Augustine is a humble man and rises as you approach, then he is a man of God and you may follow him. If he does not, but despises you, then you may despise him.' In the taut atmosphere of a synod on the Welsh border, the Celts approached Augustine. The saint remained in his seat. The Britons refused to join with the Catholic Church. Augustine was furious and threatened them with a prophecy that if they refused to worship as the English did, then they would fall victim to English swords.

Augustine's promise was fulfilled at the battle of Chester. As the Northumbrians prepared to assault the Romano-British city, their Anglo-Saxon warlord observed a large group of Celtic monks from a monastery in Bangor. The holy men had gathered to offer up prayers for the British warriors. They were guaranteed protection by a Welsh warrior called

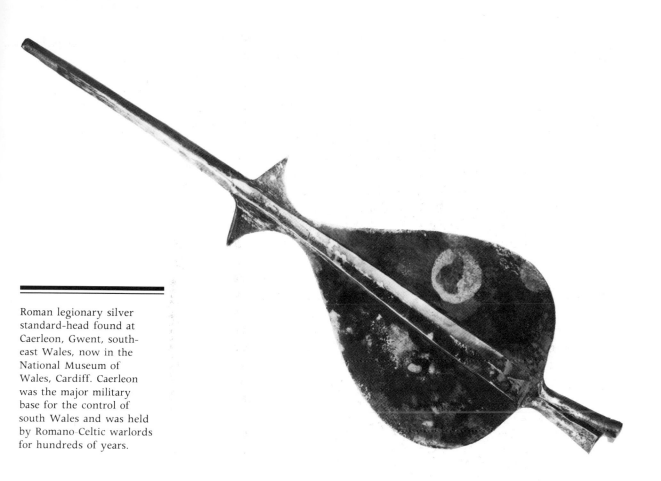

Roman legionary silver
standard-head found at
Caerleon, Gwent, south-
east Wales, now in the
National Museum of
Wales, Cardiff. Caerleon
was the major military
base for the control of
south Wales and was held
by Romano-Celtic warlords
for hundreds of years.

Brocmail. Their Celtic chants irritated the Northumbrians beyond endurance. 'Though they carry no arms,' the Angle warlord announced,
'those monks, by crying to their God, still fight against us.' Full of the
righteous fury of a Catholic charging down a heretic, the Anglo-Saxons
spurred on their horses and ploughed into the crowded monks. Brocmail
had already fled at the sight of the onrushing Northumbrians. Twelve
hundred holy men were massacred. 'Thus was fulfilled the prediction of the
holy bishop Augustine,' concludes the Anglo-Saxon chronicler Bede.

Campaigns against the Anglo-Saxons in the sixth and seventh centuries
were not the only battles the British had to fight. Romano-British warlords
along the coasts of the West Country, Wales, and north-west England had
to contend with the sea-borne raids of the Irish. These Celtic adventurers
were called *Scotti*: a name probably derived from the Irish verb 'to
plunder'. The kidnapping of St. Patrick was the most notable of their hit-
and-run exploits. In earlier centuries, Roman forts had been raised against
the pirates and much Roman bullion has been uncovered in Ireland. Some of

it includes elaborate metalwork that has been chopped up, suggesting a booty divided to pay a marauding gang. However, it is just as likely that the Irish were such a problem that the Romans gave them silver and gold as a protection payment to keep them away from their coasts. Perhaps also Irish warbands were hired by Romano-British warlords as auxiliaries.

In later centuries, the Irish were settled on coastal territories by the British as a buffer against further raids. But, like the Saxons in eastern England, they exploited the agreement and expanded their authority over British land until in the fifth century there were strong Irish realms in south-west and north-west Wales. Some British legends report that Romano-British warlords were able to expel the Scots from Anglesey and Pembrokeshire at around the same time as Arthur battled against the Saxons. But Irish presence remained potent in south Wales for some time. In Llangors Lake at Brecon, there are remains of a lake-dwelling similar to those found throughout Ireland. These crannogs were fortified settlements built upon man-made islands in the middle of swamps and lakes. Nowhere, however, was the influence of the Irish stronger than in Scotland. There they settled the craggy north-west peninsulas and imposed their language and culture on the native Britons and Picts until the very land bore their name.

Facsimile drawings of Romano-Celtic soldiers illustrated in the fifth-century manuscript of Prudentius in the National Library of Paris. Warriors such as these defended the Romano-Celtic provinces of western Europe against the Germanic barbarians.

Booty from the Anglo-Saxon wars against the Britons. A ceremonial whetstone surmounted by a bronze stag, thought to be a sceptre from the Celtic regions of north west Britain. Found in the Seventh century tomb of the Anglo-Saxon warlord of Sutton Hoo, perhaps included as a symbol of Anglo-Saxon triumph over the Celts.

The Irish, like all coastal Celts, were excellent seamen. The Irish Sea was not so much a barrier as a great lake across which trading and raiding was effectively carried. Indeed, before the establishment of a road system in Britain, communications were more efficient across water than across land. The most characteristic Celtic boat is the curach. In its simplest form, this consists of a wicker framework over which hides are stretched. That these were sea-worthy is attested by Gildas, who writes of the Picts and Scots using them to raid southern Britain. Fleets of fifty curachs are also mentioned by ancient annals. In 891, the *Anglo-Saxon Chronicle* states that 'three Irishmen came to King Alfred in a boat without a rudder, from Ireland whence they had made their way secretly because they wished for the love of God to be in a foreign land. It was made of two and a half hides and they carried with them food for seven days. And after seven days they came to land in Cornwall and went immediately to King Alfred.' Such accounts probably exaggerate the fragility of Celtic voyages, as most Celtic sea-going boats would have been more sophisticated craft like those of the Bretons, furnished with sails and steering oars. For raiding, the Irish may also have employed narrow-beamed, oak clinker-built rowing boats similar to those of the North Sea pirates.

The Irish settlement in north west Scotland was called Dalriada. At first, it was ruled by kings living in northern Ireland, but then in the fifth century Ulster warlords sailed over to Dalriada and founded an independent line of Scots kings. These Irish warriors spoke Gaelic. Dunadd became a principal stronghold. Sited on a rocky outcrop and surrounded by bogland, it recalled the hillforts of ancient times. It consisted of an inner citadel, almost a keep, in which lived the Dalriadic warlords with their retainers. Outside, in a series of courtyards formed by the rock, sheltered the labourers, peasants and animals. For centuries, the Scots and Picts battled over the highlands, often employing Britons from the lowlands against each other. The Picts were an ancient race. They spoke a language combining Celtic with an older aboriginal tongue. Their name derives from the Latin meaning 'the painted people' and refers to their custom of daubing or tattooing their bodies with woad, a blue plant dye. By the fifth century, however, this custom appears to have been neglected. The Picts were the descendants of those Caledonian tribes defeated by the Roman governor Agricola at Mons Graupius in the first century. Nevertheless, after this show of strength, the Picts remained untamed enough to prevent the Romans ever again subduing them and the province of Britain never extended into highland Scotland. Their realm survived uncontested until the arrival of the Scots.

Though their literature remains largely indecipherable, there are many Pict remains demonstrating their military might. Inscribed stone monuments show that, like all Celts, they were keen horsemen. Battlefield encounters began with horse-warriors raining javelins upon each other. They then closed in with long stout lances. Foot-soldiers fought with spears

51

and square shields and one cross-slab in Angus suggests they countered horsemen with a kind of phalanx in which warriors holding pikes stood behind shield-carriers. Some of the formidable fortresses of the Picts have been uncovered. Early in their history, they probably made use of brochs, circular towers of dry stone-work. These brochs lacked any apertures apart from the entrance and were probably solely defensive refuges against Irish pirates and Romano-British slave-raiders who could not afford a long siege. More aggressive are the major Pict fortresses with timber-laced stone walls. These possessed defendable parapets and were centres of power from which raids could be led. Curiously, these stone and timber forts resulted in the vitrification of their silica-rich foundations. For whenever they were set alight by enemies the intense heat produced by the draught channels of the timber constructions turned the stone to glass. As these forts were used over and over again, the vitrified walls no doubt formed a strong part of the defences.

The border conflicts between the Picts and the Scots of Dalriada raged for centuries. Sometimes it was the Picts who were victorious. In 740, the *Annals of Ulster* shudder at a devastating attack on Dalriada by Angus mac Fergus. He captured their strongholds and drowned a Scots warlord in triumphant execution, forcing others to row back to Ireland. But then, under a fresh generation of warriors, the Scots struck back deep into Pictland. Hoping to exploit the dissension amongst the highland Celts, the Angles of north-east England pushed up past the Britons of Strathclyde. At Nechtansmere in 685, they were met by a Pict army and so soundly thrashed that the Angles never again ventured into the Celtic highlands. Eventually, however, it was the Scots who triumphed: partly in peace, partly in war. Ever since Angus mac Fergus plunged into Dalriada, it seems that Pictish noblemen were active in Scots circles and vice versa. There were Dalriadic kings with Pictish names in the late eighth century and through such aristocratic contacts and intermarriage, the Scots King Kenneth mac Alpin succeeded to the Pictish throne around 843. No doubt it was not wholly peaceful and one tradition maintains that it was a bloody coup d'état in which the Scots wiped out Pict warbands weakened by fighting against the Vikings. Whatever the truth, from this time on the two people were united, with the Scots predominating and the Picts becoming a people of the past.

In lowland Scotland, between the rambling remains of the Antonine Wall and Hadrian's Wall, lived the Britons of Strathclyde. In former times, when the Roman walls were patrolled by warriors from all over Europe, the native Celts were allowed to rule their own territory. Only partly subdued by the Romans, it was hoped they would absorb Pict raids before they touched any Roman citizens. With the breakdown of a centralized Roman military command, the defence of the walls and their many forts was assumed by tribal warlords who had served with the Romans and ruled the surrounding territory. Rival families controlled opposite ends of the walls. At the

53

beginning of the fifth century, it was a Romano-British warlord Coel Hen—the Old King Cole of the nursery rhymes—who dominated the eastern end of the walls down to York. Combating the ever more ambitious raids of the Picts, Coel Hen followed Roman practice and employed Anglian warriors from across the North Sea. Their military settlements probably pre-date those of the Saxons. From this time on, it was not so much the crumbling Roman walls that divided enemies, but the natural bulwark of the Pennines that separated the major western and eastern powers of northern Britain. By the late sixth century, the Angles had asserted themselves and challenged the north-eastern Britons. One clash in this struggle is recorded in a Welsh poem by Aneirin. It recalls the heroes of the Gododdin.

The Romano-British Gododdin controlled the eastern end of the Antonine Wall and their power-base may have been at Edinburgh. At the time of Aneirin's poem, around 600, they were ruled by a warlord called Mynydogg. For a year before his campaign against the Angles, Mynydogg feasted his followers on mead and wine. This probably refers to a time of preparation and recruitment. For, throughout the poem, the fighting services of his men are said to be given in payment for mead. The mead and wine that a warrior received from his lord becomes a symbol of the material bond and obligation between the two. 'The war-band of Mynydogg, famous in battle,' proclaims Aneirin, 'they paid for their mead-feast with their lives.' Later the poet recalls the action of one particular hero: 'In return for mead in the hall and drink of wine, he hurled his spears between the armies.' It may be that these warriors even drank a draught of mead before battle, both to fortify themselves for conflict and to signify their loyalty to their lord. Such drinking, however, may have affected their performance in battle, as one translation suggests:

> To Nudd, the son of Ceido.
> I loved him who fell at the onset of battle,
> The result of mead in the hall and the beverage of wine.
> I loved him who blasphemed not upon the blade
> Before he was slain by Uffin.
> I loved to praise him who fed the bloodstains.
> He used his sword with animation.
> We do not speak of heroism before the Gododdin
> Without praising the son of Ceido, as one of the heroes
> of conflict.

Aneirin's poem is not a narrative but a series of panegyrics praising individual heroes who fell at the battle of Cattraeth in Yorkshire. Mynydogg assembled three hundred horse-warriors from noble families throughout northern Britain and rode them south against the Angles of Northumbria. Some of the horsemen may even have been professional freelance warriors from the highlands and north Wales. They were well equipped, mail-clad, and wore gold torques around their necks. Wealthy as they were,

Fanciful illustration of an ancient Pict with body tattoos. Engraved by Theodor de Bry after a drawing by John White, from the 1590 edition of Thomas Harriot's *The New Found Land of Virginia*. The intention was to show that the British had once been as barbaric as the native Americans were believed to be in the late sixteenth century.

T·B·J·

each warrior would have been accompanied by several retainers on spare horses. The entire war-band was therefore considerably larger than the three hundred named warriors. Whatever its strength, however, it came to grief at the battle of Cattraeth. Virtually all the three hundred leading Celtic warriors were slaughtered.

With the Gododdin shattered, north-east England and lowland Scotland were absorbed into Northumbria. Across the Pennines, however, the Britons of Cumbria and Strathclyde proved stubborn, and bitterly contested any further conquests. Around Carlisle, in the territory of the Rheged, arose an Arthur of the north-west. Urien was a warlord of the sixth century and is featured in a cycle of Welsh poems. They tell of his fight against the Angles and culminate with his death in battle. The poet Llywarch Hen imagines himself a warrior carrying away Urien's head:

> A head I carry at my side:
> The head of Urien, a generous leader of his war-band.
> On his white chest now, a black raven is perched.
> A head I carry in my cloak:
> The head of Urien, generous ruler of his court.
> On his white chest ravens glut themselves.
> A head I carry in my hand:
> He was the shepherd of Erechwydd
> Noble in heart, a spender of spears.
> A head I carry on my thigh:
> He was a shield to his land, a wheel in battle.
> He was a pillar in conflict, a snare for the enemy.
> A head I carry from the land of Pennog:
> Far reaching was his fighting.
> The head of Urien, eloquent and famous.
> A head I carry from my arm:
> He made a pile of biers out of the Angles of Bernicia.
> A head I carry in my hand:
> The head of the pillar of Britain has been toppled.
> My arm has become numb.
> My breast beats.
> My heart has broken.
> I carry the head of one that supported me.
> A head I carry on my shoulder.
> Disgrace did not overawe me.
> But woe to my hand for striking the head off my lord.

The Celtic warrior had cut the head off his slain lord so as to prevent the Angles from mutilating it.

Carlisle was a Roman city near the western end of Hadrian's Wall. It remained an important centre of Romano-British culture and would have been a focus for much Celtic resistance. A seventh-century poem announ-

Part of a hoard of gold-alloy torques discovered in Ipswich, south-east England, now in the British Museum, London. Torques may have been the badge of the free-born male and were still being worn by Celtic warlords in the sixth century, according to Aneirin.

ced that its original walls were still standing and it boasted a marvellous Roman fountain. But this was recorded by an Anglo-Saxon and it was in this century that Anglo-Saxon expansion reached its zenith, impinging yet further on the border lands. Their conquests were strengthened by a series of dynamic kings and there was little hope of a Celtic counter-attack. But still the Britons held on. In the eighth century remained the Celtic realms of Cornwall, Wales, Cumbria, Strathclyde, and Scotland. Ireland was untouched. The battle for Britain had ended in stale-mate. Half the country belonged to Germanic warlords, the rest to Celtic warlords. That the Anglo-Saxons possessed the most desirable lowland territory is significant of their

upper hand in the conflict and aided the development of their culture. A lowland cereal-based output is capable of supporting a strong church, a money economy, and centralised royal authority. Amongst the herdsmen of the Celtic highlands—where a man's wealth was measured in cattle and sheep—tribal institutions prevailed. Had the Celts already lost the economic war? It certainly seems that the Anglo-Saxons were content with their conquests and under Offa, King of Mercia, the boundary with Wales was given physical permanence. He erected a great length of earthworks, longer than Hadrian's Wall, stretching from Treuddyn to Chepstow. Not so much a fortified wall, Offa's Dyke was intended more as a boundary marker and a discouragement to cattle raiders.

Behind the ramparts of Offa's Dyke, the warlords of Wales coalesced into several regions of power. In the north, incorporating the fecund island of Anglesey, emerged the land of Gwynedd, the dominant realm of Wales. Sometimes it allied with the Mercians against the Northumbrians and a victory of the Gwynedd warlord Cadwallon was remembered as one of the Three Pollutions of the Severn as the blood of the defeated Saxons reddened

Bronze penannular brooch, originally enamelled, sixth or seventh century. From Navan Fort, County Armagh, northern Ireland, now in the British Museum, London.

the river from source to estuary. In the north-east, on the border with Mercia, was Powys. Since the Saxons had conquered the land around Chester in the seventh century, direct links between the Welsh and the Welsh-speaking Britons of Cumbria had been broken. In the south of Wales there were several principalities, such as Gwent in the south-east and Dyfed in Pembroke, whose aristocratic families claimed descent from Magnus Maximus.

By the end of the eighth century, the British status quo was shaken. The Anglo-Saxon enjoyment of their conquests was cut short by the arrival of another sea-borne invader. This was a force that would absorb half the Anglo-Saxon kingdoms, ravage the Celtic realms of Britain, and achieve what no other continental power had so far managed: the invasion of Ireland. These warriors were the Vikings.

The Northern Menace

At first the pagan Vikings came as raiders. The *Annals of Ulster* chart their progress:

AD **793.** Devastation of all the islands of Britain by gentiles.

AD **794.** The burning of Rathlin by the gentiles. The Isle of Skye was pillaged and wasted.

AD **797.** The burning of the Isle of Man by gentiles. They carried off plunder from the district. The shrine of Dochonna was broken into and other great devastations were committed by them in Ireland and Scotland.

AD **801.** Iona was burnt by gentiles.

AD **805.** The monastic community of Iona slain by gentiles, that is, sixty eight monks.

AD **806.** The gentiles burn Inishmurray and invade Roscommon.

AD **810.** A slaughter of the gentiles by the men of Antrim and Down.

AD **811.** A slaughter of the men of Connemara by the gentiles. A slaughter of the gentiles by the men of Owles and Munster.

AD **812.** A slaughter of the men of Owles by the gentiles in which was slain the king of Owles.

AD **820.** Plundering of Howth by the gentiles. A great booty of women being taken.

AD **822.** The gentiles invade Bangor in County Down.

AD **823.** The plundering of Bangor by the Foreigners and the destruction of its places of worship. The relics of Comghall were shaken out of their shrine.

Etgal, monk of the Isle of Skellig, was carried off by the gentiles and died soon after of hunger and thirst.

AD **824.** Plundering of Downpatrick by the gentiles. Burning of Moville and its places of worship. A victory of the men of Antrim and Down over the gentiles in which a great many were slain. A victory over the men of Leinster by gentiles. The martyrdom of Blamacc, son of Flann, by gentiles.

AD **826.** The plundering and burning of Lusk. The destruction of Derry to Ochta-Ugan. The destruction of the camp of the Leinstermen by gentiles, where Conall, son of Cuchongult, king of the Forthuatha, and others innumerable, were slain. A royal meeting at Birr between the king of Munster and the high king of all Ireland.

. . . and so on, from raids on coastal islands to full-scale invasions of the mainland. With each new assault, the Vikings gained more knowledge of their victims' homeland and plunged ever deeper. When their longboats could travel no further along rivers or lochs, the sea-wolves took to horses to ravage the land. Ireland was the last Celtic realm to be invaded from the continent, the last to reel before the iron blades of professional warrior-pirates. As the Vikings grew bolder, so did the size of their expeditions, until vast invading armies—intent on permanent settlement—sailed into the Irish Sea.

'There were countless sea-vomitings of ships and boats,' wrote the chronicler of the Wars of the Gaedhil (the Irish) with the Gaill (the Vikings) in the early tenth century. 'Not one harbour or landing-port or fortress in all of Munster was without fleets of Danes and pirates. There came the fleet of Oiberd and the fleet of Oduinn, and the fleets of Griffin, Snuatgar, Lagmann, Erolf, Sitriuc, Buidnin, Birndin, Liagrislach, Toirberdach, Eoan Barun, Milid Buu, Suimin, Suainin, and lastly the fleet of the Inghen Ruaidh. All the evil Ireland had so far suffered was as nothing compared to the evil inflicted by these men. The whole of Munster was plundered. They built fortresses and landing-ports all over Ireland. They made spoil-land and sword-land. They ravaged Ireland's churches and sanctuaries and destroyed her reliquaries and books. They killed Ireland's kings and chieftains and champion warriors. They enslaved our blooming, lively women, taking them over the broad green sea.'

Elsewhere in Celtic Britain, the Vikings proved equally rapacious. Scandinavian interest was first shown in the northern islands of Scotland. 'Picts and Gaelic priests were the original inhabitants of these islands,' wrote a Norwegian chronicler. 'The Picts were scarcely more than pygmies in stature, labouring strongly in the morning and evening at building their towns, but at midday they lost all their strength and out of sheer terror hid themselves in subterranean dwellings.' These dwellings may well have been the windowless stone brochs erected by Scottish natives against sea-raiders. By 800, the Norse were in firm control of the Orkneys and Shetland and sailing southwards. Though mainland Scotland was assaulted, it was largely

the Western Isles down to Man that were favoured as Viking haunts. Not all Norwegian settlement was violent and many Scandinavian farmer-fishermen lived alongside the native Celts. But, that said, it was the Vikings that dominated the Irish Sea. From their island bases, the Norse and the Danes ravaged north-west Britain and Wales. The Britons of Strathclyde and Cumbria were defeated and the Vikings tried to link their conquests around York to their bases in Ireland. On the north-west coast of England, a fierce combination of Norse and Irish set up the Viking kingdom of Galloway. In Wales, however, the Vikings bit off more than they could chew. Their raids in the 790s were repelled with heavy losses.

At this time, Wales was an assembly of little Celtic kingdoms, but it had the good fortune to be ruled by several effective warlords. In the north swelled the kingdom of Gwynedd. Its royal line claimed connections with Urien of Rheged and Coel Hen. Around the middle of the ninth century arose a warrior-lord the equal of his forefathers: Rhodri Mawr—Rhodri the Great. In 855 the Vikings made a powerful attack on the island of Anglesey, long admired as the granary of north Wales. This was to be no pushover. Rhodri responded with strength and assurance and threw the pirates out of Anglesey in a great battle. The Danish chieftain was killed. So momentus was this victory—the first major reversal of the Vikings in Britain—that it was recorded in the *Annals of Ulster* and celebrated in the court of the

'They made spoil-land and sword-land. They enslaved our blooming, lively women, taking them over the broad green sea.' A plundering expedition by Vikings. From Ward Lock's *Illustrated History of the World*, 1885.

62

Carolingians, also hard pressed by the Danes. Later though, Rhodri was savaged by the Vikings and fled to Ireland.

Welsh resistance remained defiant and there were no Scandinavian settlements in Wales. In the tenth century, Rhodri's grandson, Hywel Dda, maintained the family's dominance of Wales and emerged as its overlord. But, unlike Rhodri, Hywel was not anti-English. He knew strength derived from alliance. Thus, by doing homage to the Saxon Athelstan he kept his borderlands free of conflict and could concentrate on protecting the coastland. So successful was the Welsh defence that its general effect was to encourage the Vikings to swerve southwards and northwards to raid England. Asserting his authority over south Wales, Hywel then co-operated fully with the Anglo-Saxons of Wessex in their battle against the pagan pirates. This Christian unity seems to have worked, shielding south-west Britain from the terrible invasions that afflicted eastern England.

Scotland was similarly blessed with stout defenders and, though its islands fell completely to the Vikings, the majority of the Scottish mainland remained free of Scandinavian colonies. It was Ireland, the Celtic realm that had remained for so long free of invasion, that suffered the most. As in Anglo-Saxon England, the Viking presence was long and influential. They erected fortifications at river mouths and these developed into towns. Dublin, Waterford, Wexford, Cork and Limerick were the key Scandinavian settlements. From them, expeditions were led by land and water into the hinterland. Up until the ninth century, Ireland was roughly divided into four great spheres of power. Ulster in the north, Connacht in the west, Leinster in the east, and Munster in the south. Dominance shifted between these regions and men owed allegiances to a variety of clans within the provinces. The arrival of the ambitious Scandinavians added another element to the internecine warfare of the Celts. Irishmen allied with Danes to fight against Irishmen allied with the Norse. Throughout, the Vikings were regarded as the superior warriors. 'Not one of the champions of the Irish was able to deliver us from the tyranny of the foreign hordes,' wrote the Irish chronicler of the *Wars of the Gaedhil with the Gaill*. 'This is because of the excellence of the foreigners' polished, treble-plaited, heavy coats of mail, their hard, strong swords, their well-rivetted long spears, and because of the greatness of their bravery and ferocity and their hunger for the pure, sweet grassland of Ireland.'

That the Vikings did not conquer the whole of Ireland was probably due to the fact that it suited them just fine to extract tribute from the inland Irish through regular raiding campaigns rather than permanent conquest. The Vikings preferred to consolidate their hold on the coastline and build up their fortified ports, frequently using them to launch raids on England and Wales. Danish and Norwegian rivalry in Ireland was intense in the ninth and tenth centuries and often the only way the Irish could damage at least one of their conquerors. But, here again, as with the Romans, the Viking invasion was far from a complete disaster for the Celts. Irish

Viking broad-bladed battle axe of the tenth or eleventh century. The Irish are said to have adopted the axe as a primary weapon after the Scandinavian settlement.

warlords still ruled the interior and they gained much materially from the coastal settlements. Not least was a great improvement in trading and first-hand experience of Viking military craft. It was from this time that the Irish are supposed to have adopted the axe as a principal weapon. This was also adopted by the Scots and may have led to the development of the long-hafted battle-axe. In Ireland, Viking swords were copied, bought, and stolen. There were Irish resistance movements and one in 902 succeeded in throwing the Norse out of Dublin. But the Vikings returned and the Irish seemed content to use them in their own political intrigues, just as the Vikings employed the Irish against each other and against the kingdoms of Britain. Typical of this Celto-Scandinavian warfare was the battle of

Celtic raiders fall upon Greek guards at the pass of Thermopylae, 279 BC.

Celtiberian chieftain and warrior break through Roman siege-works surrounding their hill-fort. Numantia, northern Spain, 133 BC.

A Belgic chariot and horse-warrior harass Roman legionaries during Caesar's expedition to Britain. South-east England, 54 BC.

A sailing ship of the Veneti is boarded by Romano-Gallic auxiliaries from the Aedui. Morbihan Bay, the Atlantic coast of France, 56 BC.

Scots highlanders in a schiltron hold their ground against English knight Sir William Deyncourt. The battle of Bannockburn, 1314.

Edward Bruce attacked by Anglo-Irish warriors at Moiry Pass in Armagh, Ulster, 1315.

Pict horse-warriors chase an isolated Scot into a deserted broch. Dalriada, north-west Scotland, seventh century.

Murchad, the son of Brian Boru, High King of all Ireland, tackles a Viking at the battle of Clontarf, Dublin, 1014.

A Norman Breton landlord is ambushed by Welsh herdsmen. The Marches of northern Wales, late eleventh century.

Dermot MacMurrogh, warlord of Leinster, is backed up by a Norman Welsh knight and a Welsh archer. Ossory, south-east Ireland, 1169.

Cuchulainn of Ulster rides his legendary scythed chariot against Connacht raiders, described in the pre-Christian Irish saga *Tain Bo Cuailnge*.

An Arthurian Romano-British landlord clashes with a Saxon raider on the outskirts of Bath, Britain, in the late fifth century.

Owain Glyndwr and his Welsh followers are attacked by the English garrison of Caernarfon Castle, 1401.

James IV, King of Scotland, is cut down by English billmen, and longbowmen. The battle of Flodden, Northumberland, 1513.

A galloglas and his kern attendants await their Irish lord, Shane O'Neill, during his visit to the court of Elizabeth I, London, 1562.

Irish warriors of the army of Hugh O'Neill charge upon the English at the battle of the Yellow Ford, Ulster, 1598.

Clontarf at the beginning of the eleventh century—a campaign that made Brian Boru's reputation as one of the greatest warlords of Ireland.

As chieftain of the Dal Cais at the mouth of the river Shannon, Brian Boru established himself through a series of guerilla attacks on the Scandinavian settlers around Limerick. 'However small the injury he might be able to do to the foreigners,' wrote the chronicler of the Gaedhil, 'Brian preferred it to peace. From the forests and wastelands, he emerged to plunder and kill the foreigners. If he did not destroy them during the day, then he was sure to do so at night. Moreover, his followers set up temporary dwellings rather than settled camps as they moved through the woods and solitudes laying waste to northern Munster. The foreigners of Tratraighe raised great fortified banks around their settlements and prepared to conquer northern Munster. But Brian killed many of the foreigners of the garrison. Great were the hardships that Brian endured: bad food and bad bedding on the wet, knotty roots of his own country. It is said that the foreigners killed many of his followers so that only 15 survived.' But, with reinforcements from other Irish warlords, Brian continued his hammering of the Vikings.

At the age of 26, Brian Boru stormed the Viking city of Limerick. The campaign had begun with the battle of Sulcoit. There, the Vikings had assembled a force of Danes and Irish. The chronicler of the *Wars of the Gaedhil* says that these Irishmen were brought under tribute, and when some Munster chieftains refused to join the Danes they were murdered. In truth, many warlords of Munster were probably only too willing to side with the powerful Vikings against the upstart Brian. The Dal Cais and Brian's fellow chieftains were none too keen to confront the superior force in open conflict, but with the arrival of a renowned Irish champion, a freelance warrior with a hundred retainers all armed and bearing large shields, they decided to fight a 'manly battle on the open part of the plain.' The Vikings were mounted and wore mail. It is likely that Brian and his chief retainers were also so armed. This was, after all, a battle between professional warriors. Numbers were not large and few unarmoured peasants would have been involved. From sunrise to midday, the warriors struck and slaughtered each other. Finally, it was the Vikings who broke and were chased by the Dal Cais 'who killed and beheaded from that time until evening.'

Brian and his warriors overran Limerick, slaughtering and plundering. 'They carried off the foreigners' jewels and their best property: their saddles beautiful and foreign; their gold and silver; their satins and silken cloth, pleasing and variegated, both scarlet and green. They carried away their soft, youthful girls, their silk-clad women, and their large and well-formed boys. The fortress and the good town they reduced to a cloud of smoke and red fire. All the captives were assembled. Every one fit for war was killed and every one else enslaved.' It seems that many of the Danish women were then ritually raped. Brian's sack of Limerick, though barbaric, showed him as a man of power. He now consolidated his success. Local

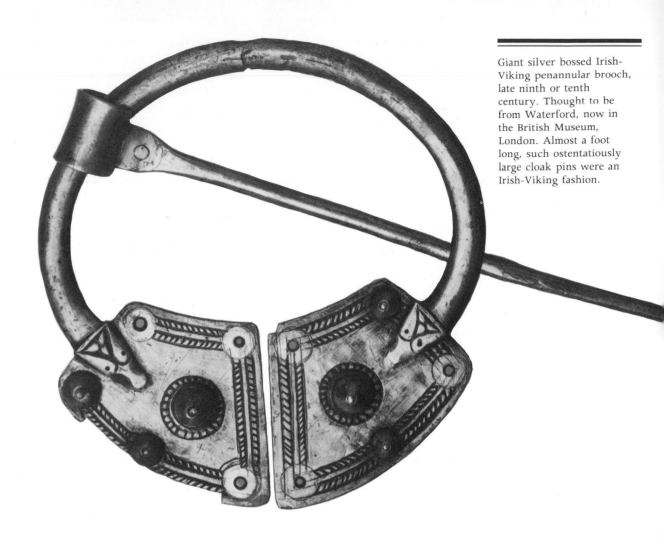

opposing chieftains were slain. His warriors kept fit and fed by numerous cattle raids. He built a fleet upon the Shannon and sailed as far as Loch Ree where he plundered the territory of Connacht and Meath. With his hold over Munster secure, Brian then moved against the men of Leinster.

The lords of Leinster appreciated the benefits of Viking colonies on their land and allied with the Vikings of Dublin against Brian. The two forces met around the year 1000 and the men of Munster were triumphant. Dublin was ransacked and the Vikings forced to submit to Brian's authority. They were allowed back into their settlement on acknowledging Brian's overlordship and no doubt ensuring he received a goodly part of their trading profits. As lord of Munster, Leinster and the Viking communities, Brian's ambitions were now focused on the north. Mustering a war-band of Irish and Danes, he rode to Tara and challenged the high king of Ireland to battle. For centuries, the clans of the north had been the dominant force in Ireland.

The O'Neills had ruled Ulster and from them descended a line of high kings of all Ireland. Now, around the year 1002, Mael Sechnaill, lord of Meath and holder of the high kingship, sent requests to all the warlords of Ulster and Connacht to counter the usurper. But the head of the northern O'Neills recognised true power and replied to Mael Sechnaill: 'Whoever possesses Tara, let them defend its freedom. It is not right that one man should risk his life against the Dal Cais in defence of sovereignty for another man.'

Mael Sechnaill offered his crown to the O'Neills. 'I would rather give thee hostages,' he told them, 'than be dependent on Brian Boru.' But they refused. Even the men of Meath, Mael Sechnaill's homeland, would not take up arms to defend him. The overawed north chose a relatively peaceful submission rather than war. At Tara, Brian assumed the high kingship of all Ireland. He followed this up with raids on all the northern estates of Ulster and Connacht, principally to obtain noble hostages but also to fill his coffers and strengthen his army. As was becoming obvious, Brian Boru's conquest of Ireland was not a nationalistic battle of Celt against Viking. It was a personal struggle to supreme power in which Irishmen fought Irishmen with the Vikings helping as auxiliaries and hoping to hang on to their colonies. Despite regular rebellions, Brian ruled as overlord of Ireland for over a decade. He even sent expeditions across the Irish Sea to levy tributes from the Scots, Welsh and Anglo-Saxons.

As Brian grew older, so his grip on Ireland weakened. In 1013, the lords of Leinster and the Vikings of Dublin threw off their allegiance to him. After a series of probing raids on each other, Brian and his son led warriors from Munster and Connacht to Dublin and set siege to it. A lack of provisions forced Brian to retire, but in the next year he returned. Plundering through Leinster, he closed on Dublin. The Vikings sent messengers throughout their territories and across the Irish Sea to gather an army. On receiving the call, fleets of adventurers set sail. The Viking warlords of Orkney and the Isle of Man arrived with their followers. They were joined by Danish and Celtic Cumbrian mercenaries. The Irishmen of north Leinster were ready for the fight, but those of the south lost their nerve and backed away.

Brian's army relied principally on the men of Munster and the Dal Cais, the heartland of his support. There were some warriors from Connacht and Meath, but Brian knew these were not to be trusted, being likely to desert in the first onslaught. There were no men from Ulster. At the last moment, Brian was joined by a group of Vikings from the Isle of Man who had hastily converted to Christianity to assure him of their support. As his forces gathered beneath striped banners of red, green and yellow, Brian sent horsemen forward to plunder all round Dublin. He thanked the warlords who had brought him men and cursed those who did not.

To stop the Irish plundering, the men of Dublin rode out from their settlement, crossed the rivers Liffey and Tolka, and set upon Brian's warriors to the north of the town in an area called Clontarf. The Vikings were brilliantly garbed in mail-coats of iron decorated with brass rings. According to the chronicler of the *Wars of the Gaedhil*, these mail-coats were triple layered. The Danes opened the fighting with their bows and arrows. 'Poisoned arrows, covered in the blood of dragons, toads, and the water-snakes of hell.' They then set to with dark spears and stout swords. According to the chronicler of the *Wars of the Gaedhil*, the Irish warriors of Brian did not wear mail, but fought in long, many-coloured tunics with shields with bronze bosses. The chieftains wore crested helmets studded with precious stones, and sound like heroes from the *Tain Bo Cuailnge*. In reality, both sides probably looked very similar, clad in mail with swords, axes and spears. Brian placed his most dependable warriors of the Dal Cais in the forefront of the battle, led by his son Murchad. Behind these were the other men of Munster. On their flanks were Brian's Viking mercenaries and Irish auxiliaries. The men of Meath, led by Mael Sechnaill, were said to have made secret contact with the Vikings of Dublin and sat out the battle behind earthworks. The Vikings of Dublin, led by the warlord Sitric, and the warriors of Leinster, led by Maelmore, placed their Danish and Norwegian auxiliaries in the front of their army. The Vikings from Orkney were led by Sigurd and those from Man by Brodar.

'The two sides made a furious, smashing onset on each other. And there arose a frightful screaming and fluttering above their heads as birds and demons awaited their prey.' At first, Brian's flank of Irish auxiliaries clashed with the Leinstermen. The Leinstermen broke and were chased off by mail-clad horsemen. It was then that the Dal Cais and the Vikings hacked at each other with axe and sword. A strong wind hampered the throwing of spears. From their walls and towers, the inhabitants of Dublin watched the men of Connacht play a key role in bloodying the Vikings. But, above all, the battle of Clontarf was a combat of individuals. A fight in which warriors could make a name for themselves: become heroes recalled in epic poems. As the crowds surged—men flailing their limbs and weapons excited by fear and violence—the sagas isolated individual combats.

Murchad, son of Brian, wielded two swords, one in his right hand and one in his left: he had equal power in striking. Enraged by the Viking slaughter of his fellow Dal Cais, Murchad rushed at the Danes like a furious ox. He made a hero's breach in the enemy. Fifty foreigners fell to his right hand; fifty foreigners fell to his left hand. One blow was sufficient to kill them. Neither shield nor mail stood up to his blades. Murchad's retainers followed their master into the heart of the battle. Such feats cowed the Vikings: many turned and ran. But Sigurd of Orkney refused to flee. Slaughtering and mutilating the Dal Cais, no point or blade seemed to harm the Norseman. Murchad rushed upon him and dealt with his right hand a crushing blow to his neck that cut the mail and straps of his helmet. Murchad then brought his left-hand sword down on the Viking's exposed neck, felling the warrior with these two blows.

Still Murchad was not finished. Fury urged his body on and he charged

Welsh iron stirrups found in Glamorgan, south Wales, late tenth century, now in the National Museum of Wales, Cardiff. Welsh warriors kept Wales relatively free of the Vikings.

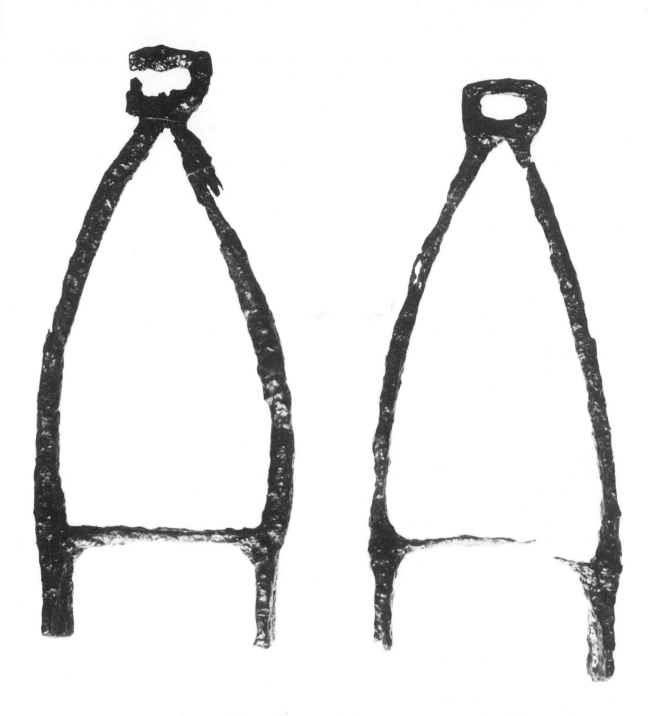

upon another Viking warlord. This time, the inlaid ornament of Murchad's sword began to melt with the heat of his striking. Throwing the burning blade away, the Irish hero gripped hold of the foreigner's armour and wrenched the mail over his head. The two warriors fell to the ground and wrestled. Murchad thrust the Viking's own sword into his ribs. But the foreigner drew his knife and ripped a gash in Murchad's guts. Exhaustion and pain overcame both warriors. They lay beside each other. But before he fainted, Murchad is said to have cut off the Viking's head. Murchad survived the night, but died the next day after taking communion and making his confession and will.

Throughout the battle, Brian took no active role in the fighting. He stayed at the rear protected by the shield-wall of his retainers, issuing orders and praying. It was there he received news of the eventual rout of the enemy and their desparate dash to the sea. But the victory was not clear-cut. Brian's army had lost many men, and in the chaos at the end of the day

Welsh horseman at the base of the Cross of Irbic. Cast of the tenth century cross in Llandough churchyard, near Penarth, south Wales. Such warriors fought alongside the Anglo-Saxons against the sea-wolves.

Viking bands still roamed around the battlefield. One, led by Brodar of Man, rode through the relaxing Irish ranks toward Brian's camp. At the height of victory, Brodar's sudden attack was unexpected and the Viking succeeded in reaching Brian himself. Brian unsheathed his sword and gave the foreigner such a blow that he cut the Viking's leg off at the knee. The Viking then dealt Brian a stroke that cleft his head in half. Thus Brian died at the moment of his greatest victory.

For a victory, the battle of Clontarf seemed like a defeat. Ireland's greatest overlord was dead and his retinue devastated. In the aftermath, Ireland reverted to a disunity of warring clans. Nevertheless, it was a decisive defeat of the Vikings: keeping Ireland free of any further Scandinavian invasions. Of course, the Vikings of Dublin and Leinster continued to live in their coastal settlements, but they operated alongside the Irish and did not dominate them. They became Christians and intermarried with the Irish noble families. Vikings from abroad still harried the coasts in search of plunder but they could expect an equally ferocious reaction from the Irish. The Heimskringla Saga of the thirteenth century recalls raids by King Magnus of Norway on the Irish coast a century earlier. Sailing from Norway to the Orkneys to the Hebrides, Magnus then harried Ireland. Along the coast of Ulster, he demanded a shore-killing of cattle to provide his warriors with fresh meat. The Irish refused: Magnus and his followers disembarked. As they penetrated inland, they readied themselves for ambush. 'King Magnus wore his helm,' wrote the chronicler, 'and a red shield displaying a lion in gold. Strapped to his side was a sword called Leg-Biter: the best of weapons. Its hilt was of walrus tooth and the handle covered in gold. Over his shirt he wore a red silk jacket with a lion sewn in gold silk on its back and front. He carried a spear.'

Apparently, the Vikings found the slaughtered cattle, but as they returned through the coastal marshes, the Irish broke cover. In the confusion, the Vikings were separated and many fell to Irish arrows. Magnus ordered a shield-wall around his standard. The Viking retreat was hindered by a dyke. Magnus was wounded: stabbed with a spear through both legs beneath the knee. He grabbed the spear and broke it off, bellowing 'Here's how we break every spear shaft, my lads!' Some of his comrades clambered over the dyke in an attempt to cover the rest, but they panicked and ran for their ships. Magnus was wounded again: a mortal blow on the neck with an Irish axe. Around him his closest retainers fell. One, called Vidkunn, managed to escape the carnage, picking up his lord's sword and standard. The Vikings sailed immediately back to Norway. At home, Vidkunn managed to avoid the terrible disgrace of surviving his lord, by showing his many wounds and insisting that he had slain all Magnus' killers. Only then did the sons of Magnus receive him with love.

Although the Vikings established enduring colonies along the coast of Ireland and in the northern and western islands of Scotland, it remains a remarkable fact that mainland Ireland, Scotland, and Wales remained relatively free of Scandinavian settlement, whereas a good half of Anglo-Saxon England was absorbed by the Danes and Norse. This may be due to the land of the Anglo-Saxons being richer and more attractive, but it must also attest to the fierce independence of the leading Celtic warlords. Such was the power of these Celtic warlords that Viking adventurers frequently found it more profitable to intervene on their side in the endless little wars of the Dark Ages. Macbeth, a Gaelic warrior from Moray, was assisted by the Vikings of Orkney in his assault upon Duncan, king of the Scots.

Macbeth has suffered badly from history. Shakespeare transformed him into an archetype of murderous medieval anarchy. In reality, it seems he was no worse and may have been better than other contemporary warlords. On seizing the crown of Scotland in 1040, he ruled the land for a prosperous 17 years. So settled was the country that he felt secure enough to leave and journey to Rome on a pilgrimage. As for Duncan: he had led his countrymen into a string of defeats. When Macbeth proclaimed himself king at Scone, few chroniclers protested. Indeed, later historians have even regarded his success as a highland Celtic reaction against the excessive English influence encouraged by Duncan. Besides, Macbeth, like Duncan, was a grandson of Malcolm II and had a legitimate claim to the throne. In Celtic clan law, election was the method of obtaining power. A more capable and popular warlord could legally oust an elder relative.

The Scotland that Macbeth ruled was a greatly extended country. In 1018, the Northumbrian Angles had been shattered at Carham by Malcolm II and he rode on to claim the lowlands as far as Hadrian's Wall. That same year, the king of the Britons of Strathclyde and Cumbria died without an heir and the triumphant Scots immediately placed Malcolm's grandson Duncan on their throne. In 1034, Duncan became King of Scotland. Six years later, he was killed by Macbeth in battle near Burghead on the Moray Firth. In that combat, Macbeth rode in an army of northern Gaelic clansmen allied with Norse warriors led by Thorfinn Sigurdsson, lord of Caithness and Orkney. It was the Vikings who took the lead in the battle, as it was they who Duncan had come to humble. Duncan fought alongside southern clansmen and Irish mercenaries. The *Orkneyinga Saga* evokes some of the conflict: 'After the crashing of spears, the Orkney warlord raised high his helmet. He exulted in battle and reddened spear point and sword edge with Irish blood. With stout arm, the gracious lord kinsman of Hlodver bore up his Welsh shield and rushed upon the enemy.' With his Irish auxiliaries routed, Duncan managed a counter-charge, but the Norse held firm and Duncan was slain amidst the fighting.

Duncan's son, Malcolm, lived as an exile in England and was brought up on that court's concepts of heredity. As Duncan's eldest son, he was convinced he was entitled to be king and not Macbeth. But Macbeth was strong and Malcolm had to bide his time. Malcolm's ambition and revenge suited the English just fine, for here was a man they could control. As soon as he reclaimed the throne, the Scottish monarchs would have to do homage

Welsh warrior with mace and dagger on the Cross of Briamail Fou. Cast of the restored tenth-century stone from Llandyfaelog Fach churchyard, Powys, north-east Wales.

to the Anglo-Saxon king and thus admit the feudal superiority of England over Scotland. It would also secure their northern borders. So, in 1054, backed up by an army of Anglo-Saxons and Danes, the 21-year-old Malcolm advanced on Scotland by land and by sea. His army was led by a Northumbrian-Danish warlord called Siward. The English met little resistance from the Scots in the lowlands and were confronted by Macbeth just outside Scone, the Scottish capital. This was the famous battle in which supposedly 'Birnam Wood do come to Dunsinane'. No doubt accompanied by his Norse allies—the lord of Orkney was his cousin—Macbeth put up a stiff fight. But the *Annals of Ulster* maintain that 3,000 Scots were killed and 1,500 English and Danes slain. Still, it was far from a victory and Siward had to withdraw his troops from Scotland, Malcolm having to be content with lordship over Cumbria.

The next year, Siward died and in 1057 Malcolm alone had to lead the battle against Macbeth. With the full support of the Northumbrians, Malcolm cornered the King of Scotland in his homeland of Moray. Macbeth and his retainers charged Malcolm's warriors but were overcome and killed. Even then, Malcolm did not immediately succeed to the throne but had to avoid the avenging highlanders and back off southwards to safety. The next year, Malcolm had to slaughter Macbeth's stepson, his legally elected successor, before the anglicised Malcolm could crown himself at Scone. With his accession came closer ties with England and a retreat in the influence of the Gaelic clansmen. Far from being a tyrant, Macbeth could be called the last of the truly Celtic kings of Scotland.

With the acceptance of Viking spheres of influence in the islands of Scotland and the cities of Ireland, there followed a short period of consolidation beneficial to both Celt and Scandinavian. This status quo was overturned at the end of the eleventh century with the arrival of another wave of North Men. This time, they did not come direct from Scandinavia, but were the French descendants of that aggressive colony of Vikings in north-west France: the Normans. In the years following their great victory of 1066, they successfully subdued the whole of England. It was not long before they then overran the borders of the British Celtic realms. In this adventure, the Normans were joined by other French warriors. Not least amongst them were the Celtic warlords of Brittany.

The Bretons had managed to hold on to their Celtic identity despite the power of the Franks. In the ninth century, they made large gains in Normandy and though beaten back, Rennes remained Breton. When Harold of England stayed with William of Normandy, he accompanied the Duke on expeditions against the Bretons. With the submission of several Breton warlords, William then included them as an important contingent in his invasion of England. At the battle of Hastings, they formed an entire flank. Highly regarded by the Normans and fighting in a similar manner, the Bretons did well out of the conquest and received extensive estates. Some were settled in the south-west and on the Welsh border where their Celtic language, similar to that of the Welsh, was of considerable help in dealing with the natives.

The Norman conquest of Wales was piecemeal. It took a long time and was never completed. Much of this difficulty has been ascribed to the rough Welsh countryside. The mountainous interior covered with forests. Heavy rainfall ensuring that the clay soil was marshy for much of the year. Above all, however, it was the quality of Welsh resistance. 'They make fine use of light arms, which do not impede their agility,' observed the twelve-century Welsh Norman writer, Giraldus Cambrensis. 'They wear short coats of mail, helmets and shields, and sometimes greaves plated with iron. They carry bundles of arrows and long spears. Their nobles ride into battle, but the majority fight on foot. In time of peace, young men learn to endure the fatigue of war by penetrating deep into the forests and climbing the mountains.' In short, the Welsh were excellent guerilla warriors. Giraldus, therefore, recommended that the Normans should also employ lightly armoured foot-soldiers, and when possible the Normans incorporated Welshmen into their own forces. But, before this, a conqueror of Wales must prepare his victim. Giraldus suggests the Normans divide the Welsh with bribes and treaties, then blockade the coasts and the English border so that few provisions reached them. In the event, the Normans chose their path of conquest carefully and exploited the Welsh geography by sticking to the wide coastal plains.

Led by adventurers hungry for land of their own, the Normans first settled Gwent in south Wales. Whenever possible, William preferred to admit the homage of native Welsh warlords, but the desire of his landless followers ensured that a slow advance began around the coasts of Wales. As always, foreign influence was aided by Celtic power-play and Welsh exiles from Ireland fought alongside the Norman knights. Bit by bit, the Norman lords of the Marches—a French word meaning frontier—encroached on Welsh territory. The Marcher lords were used by successive English kings as a means of creating buffer states between themselves and the Welsh. They were offered absolute power over any frontier land they could subdue. It was an offer the warrior families of the Fitzalans, Gilberts, Clares, Mortimers and Laccys could not refuse. At the head of their war-bands, supported by the border garrisons of Chester, Shrewsbury, Hereford and Bristol, they carved out private kingdoms where their word was law.

Fierce resistance rocked the invaders from the end of the eleventh century. Woodcutting pioneers had to advance before Norman war-bands, clearing away undergrowth that might hide Welsh guerillas. The Marcher lords managed to hold onto many of their conquests and even north-west Wales, the heartland of the powerful dynasty of Gwynedd, lay at times in their hands. But, recovering from the shock of the Norman war-machine, the Welsh had begun to fight back and much of northern and central Wales remained solidly Celtic. Two centuries of raid and counter-raid now followed: the borders becoming a wilderness of slaughter. In a constant

Celtic Bretons fought alongside the Normans at the battle of Hastings and gained much from the share-out. Hand-coloured engraving from Charles Stothard's *Bayeux Tapestry* published in 1819.

state of war, the Marcher lords grew in power and frequently had to be quelled by their own king. The Welsh in their turn became hardened and Gwynedd was re-established from Anglesey down the west coast. By 1137, Gwynedd was recognised by the Norman English as the chief Celtic realm of Wales, so Welshmen could proclaim: 'No other language but Welsh shall answer for this land on the day of Judgement.' The Welsh had defied the initial onslaught of the mighty Normans.

Scotland became the home for many English refugees of the Norman conquest. Malcolm III married the sister of Edgar Aetheling, the only surviving claimant to the Anglo-Saxon throne after Harold. Again, this brought increased anglicisation and the Celtic Church of Scotland fell in line with the Church of Rome. Malcolm was persuaded to support Saxon claims to the English throne and four times he invaded Northumbria. By 1072, William tired of this aggression and led an army north. He forced Malcolm to accept him as overlord. But, with William's death, the Scots again ravaged Northumbria. The Conqueror's son, William Rufus, countered swift and hard. In the fighting, he took Cumbria as far as Carlisle, thus establishing Scotland's frontier as it has remained ever after. It was in another raid across the border that Malcolm was killed by a Norman knight. His death encouraged a Gaelic backlash and a warlord from the Hebrides was elected king of Scotland at Scone. The English followers of Malcolm were expelled.

The Normans could not rest with such a state of affairs. Over the next stormy years, Norman-backed claimants proclaimed their crowning as an hereditary right against the old Celtic system of election. Eventually the Anglo-Norman kings triumphed and the Celtic way of life retreated to the highlands. Scots sympathetic to England and new Norman landlords infiltrated the lowlands. In peace, the Normans gained much more Scottish territory than they would have won from battle. Gaelic was still spoken by the common people of Scotland, especially the almost independent clan-lords of the north, but Norman-French became the dominant language of the Scottish aristocracy. Some refugees of the old regime fled to Ireland. There they joined with the Vikings of Dublin in raids against the west coasts of Britain. It may have been such conflict that encouraged certain Welsh Norman warlords to look across the Irish channel with ambition.

No one likes to commit to history the fact that his people have invaded another country out of sheer lust for conquest. Caesar justified his invasion of Celtic France as an intervention on behalf of the Gauls against the Germans. When Giraldus Cambrensis came to write his history of the Norman expedition to Ireland, he too opened his account with an invitation. The unity to be expected from the great victory at Clontarf in 1014 had come to nothing with the death of Brian. Ireland in the twelfth century was divided by bitter dynastic feuds. Leinster, always ready to do business with foreigners, was led by Dermot MacMurrough. Now Dermot had abducted the wife of Tiernan O'Rourke and in a revenge worthy of the Trojan War, O'Rourke and Rory O'Connor of Connacht, high king of Ireland, was coming to get him.

In 1166, Dermot sailed for help to the Norman court of Henry II. The king agreed to aid the Irishman as 'vassal and liegeman', but could not afford to send his own troops. Instead, Dermot was allowed permission to recruit the support of the Marcher lords of south Wales. Frustrated by the resurgence of the Welsh, many warriors were keen to join Dermot. They were led by the half-Norman, half-Welsh Robert FitzStephen who agreed to help Dermot in return for the town of Wexford as payment. By 1169, FitzStephen had disembarked at Bannow Bay in Leinster with thirty fully-armoured retainers, sixty half-armoured horsemen, and three hundred archers and foot-soldiers, all from south Wales. A force more Celtic than Norman, although the Annals of Tighernach say that the majority of soldiers were Flemish immigrants from settlements in Wales. Wishing to secure his promised land, FitzStephen wasted no time and made straight for Wexford. One of the major Viking settlements, Wexford was still ruled by Norse-Irish and considered itself independent from Leinster. The townsmen resolved to battle it out and advanced to meet the Norman army now joined by Irish warriors sent by Dermot. But the men of Wexford were overawed by the Norman horsemen and their armour, and retreated back into their town, burning all the outlying buildings.

The English defeat at Hastings in 1066 had profound repercussions for all of Celtic Britain. The death of king Harold engraved for Cassell's *History of England*, 1875.

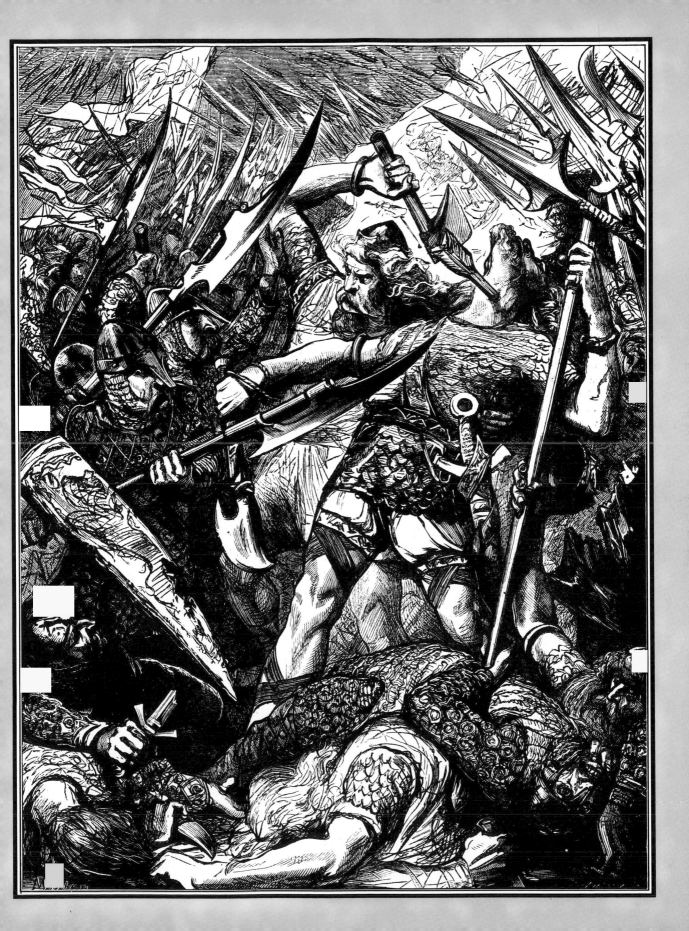

Throughout his account, Giraldus Cambrensis emphasises the military primitiveness of the Irish. 'They go to battle without armour,' he writes, 'considering it a burden and esteeming it brave to fight without it. They are armed with three kinds of weapons: short spears, light darts, and heavy battle-axes of iron, exceedingly well wrought and tempered. These they borrowed from the Norwegians. In striking with the battle-axe they use only one hand, instead of both. When all other weapons fail, they hurl stones against the enemy. In riding, they use neither saddles, nor boots, nor spurs, but carry only a rod in their hand with which they urge forward their horses.' Latin propaganda seems uppermost here, for in reality, the Irish nobility and certainly the Scandinavian Irish were as well equipped as the Normans and wore similar long coats of mail, iron helmets with nasal, and kite-shaped shields. And always, the Celtic Irish were excellent horsemen.

It is in Giraldus' contemptuous descriptions that we see the origin of the English prejudice against the Irish and their belief in the inferiority of Irish culture. 'Their clothes are made after a barbarous fashion,' he continues. 'Their custom is to wear small close-fitting hoods, hanging below the shoulders. Under this they use woollen rugs instead of cloaks, with breeches and hose of one piece, usually dyed. The Irish are a rude people, subsisting on the produce of their cattle only and living like beasts. This people, then, is truly barbarous, being not only barbarous in their dress, but suffering their hair and beards to grow enormously in an uncouth manner.'

FitzStephen lost no time in preparing for his assault on Wexford. His armoured warriors moved into the dry trenches around the city, while his archers covered them by raking the wall-towers. The Normans then heaved their siege ladders against the walls and clambered to the top with loud cries. The men of Wexford cast down large stones and wooden beams and managed to repulse the attack. With only a few hundred men under his command, FitzStephen called off the assault and withdrew to the harbour where he set fire to all the ships. Undeterred, the next morning, after celebrating mass, the Normans assaulted the walls again. This time, the townsmen despaired of holding the battlements and preferred to make a peaceful settlement. With bishops acting as mediators, the town did homage to Dermot and he in turn gave the town and its surrounding countryside to FitzStephen. The townsmen now joined the Normans and Leinstermen on their freebooting and ravaged the territory of Ossory. At the end of this raiding campaign, fought by horsemen amid woods and bogs, two hundred heads were laid at the feet of Dermot. He turned the heads one by one, raising his hands in joy as he recognised those of his enemies. 'Among them was one he hated above all others,' wrote Giraldus, 'and taking it up by the ears and hair, he tore the nostrils and lips with his teeth in a most savage and inhuman way.'

Receiving the homage of the lord of Ossory, Dermot was now perceived

Stone keep of Cardiff
Castle built by Robert,
Duke of Gloucester,
between 1121 and 1147.
The Welsh called the
Normans 'the castle men'
as they used their motte
and bailey fortresses to
subdue the Celts. But in
1158, Ifor Bach, the Welsh
lord of Senghenydd, scaled
the walls of Cardiff castle
and kidnapped the
then Norman lord of
Glamorgan and held him
ransom.

as a threat by Rory O'Connor, the high king. As the men of Connacht rode out against Dermot, he, under FitzStephen's direction, prepared a defensive position among the thick woods and bogs of Leinster. Trees were felled, underwood cut and woven into hedges, level ground broken up with holes and trenches, and secret passages cut through thickets. Hidden away thus, Dermot avoided a major conflict and instead offered to reassert his submission to Rory and give him hostages. The Normans would be sent away as soon as they helped Dermot secure Leinster. This apparently assured Rory and there was peace. But no sooner had the high king retreated than Maurice FitzGerald landed at Wexford with 140 Norman-Welsh warriors. While FitzStephen erected a fort of earth ramparts and wood stockade at Wexford, Dermot and FitzGerald marched on Dublin. They ravaged and burned the territory around Dublin so the Norse governors were compelled to accept Dermot's lordship. Dermot now sent

FitzStephen to the aid of the lord of Limerick and north Munster and they raided the land of Rory O'Connor. This was reckless indeed, but, with his Norman allies, Dermot now entertained thoughts of snatching the high kingship. On the advice of FitzStephen and FitzGerald, Dermot sent to England for more warriors. Above all, he requested the help of Richard FitzGilbert, a powerful Norman warlord of south Wales nicknamed Strongbow.

The special character of warfare in medieval Ireland is described fully by Giraldus Cambrensis. 'The Normans may be very good soldiers in their own country,' he wrote, 'expert in the use of arms and armour in the French manner, but every one knows how much that differs from the way of war in Ireland and Wales. In France, war is carried out across open plains; here, you find dense woods and mountainous terrain. In France, it is counted an honour to wear armour; here, it is a burden. There, victories are won by close fighting ranks; here, by the charges of lightly armed warriors. There, quarter is given and prisoners offered for ransom; here, heads are chopped off as trophies and no one escapes. Therefore, in all expeditions in Ireland and Wales, the Welshmen bred in the Marches make the best troops. They are good horsemen and light on foot. They can bear hunger and thirst well when provisions are not to be had. These are the men who took the lead in the conquest of Ireland and will be needed to complete it. For when you have to deal with a race naturally agile and whose haunts are in rocky places, you need lightly armed troops. In addition, in the Irish wars, particular care should be taken to include archers for they can counter the Irishmen who rush forward and throw stones at our heavily armoured warriors and then retreat.' It may be said that the Normans in England by the twelfth century should properly be called English for they were long descended from those Normans of 1066. This is true, but what is clear from Giraldus' passage above is that these warriors still considered themselves fighting in a Norman French manner different from that of the native Celts of Britain. Hence their dependence on Welsh auxiliaries.

In 1170, Strongbow arrived in Ireland. He brought with him 200 armoured horsemen and 1,000 Welsh archers and other soldiers. He had already sent an advance group of warriors and they had set up a beach-head near Waterford. The Viking-Irish townsmen savaged this advance guard and when Strongbow landed he made straight for them. Surveying the walls of Waterford, the Normans spotted a little wooden house on the outside attached to the stockade. This in turn was being supported by a single post. Under cover of their archers, armoured warriors rushed into the house and chopped down the pole. As the house collapsed, it brought with it part of the town wall. The Normans clambered over the wreckage and burst into the town. Some of the leading citizens held out in a tall stone tower but eventually they were overcome. Joined by Dermot, FitzStephen and FitzGerald, Strongbow now rode on Dublin. They descended unexpectedly by a mountain track and the Viking lord of Dublin immediately entered into lengthy peace negotiations. While they talked, a group of Normans stormed the walls.

Heady with success, Dermot raided the territory of his greatest enemy: Tiernan O'Rourke. Rory O'Connor reminded Dermot of his peace agreement but not even the execution of his own son, kept hostage by Rory, could prevent Dermot's ambition and he now claimed the high kingship. But Dermot's luck had run out. A few months later he died, leaving Strongbow in command of Leinster and the Viking towns. This did not please king Henry II of England who feared a warlord grown too powerful. He ordered the Normans to return on penalty of losing their lands in England and refused to allow any ship to sail to Ireland. This loss of reinforcements and supplies fell hard on Strongbow but he held his conquered territories.

In the meantime, Haskulf, the Viking lord of Dublin, returned to his city with sixty ships full of Northmen from the Isle of Man and the Scottish Isles. 'They were under the command of John the Mad,' reported Giraldus. 'Some wore long breastplates, others shirts of mail. Their shields were round, coloured red, and bound with iron. They were lion-hearted and iron-armed men. A member of the garrison had his leg cut off by a single stroke of one of their battle-axes.' The Normans were bundled back into Dublin. They regrouped, however, and a contingent moved out unobserved and pounced upon the rear of the besieging Vikings. The Northmen were thrown into confusion and routed. In order to calm the still largely Scandinavian townspeople, Haskulf, though a prisoner, was brought back in triumph to Dublin. Before the Norman lord of the city, he did not thank him for his mercy but insisted: 'We came as a small band, but if my life is spared, we will follow up with a much more formidable assault.' Haskulf was beheaded.

Hoping to exploit Strongbow's isolated situation, the Irish now besieged Dublin. While a Viking fleet blockaded the port of the city, Rory O'Connor assembled his men of Connacht and Meath, and supporters from Leinster and Ulster. Even worse for Strongbow was the fact that FitzStephen was surrounded in his castle by the men of Wexford. For two months the siege of Dublin persisted. With food running low and no prospect of relief, the Normans decided to bring the struggle to a head. 'What are we waiting for?' asked FitzGerald of his comrades. 'Do we expect help from our homeland? No. Such is our situation that to the Irish, we are English, and to the English, we are Irish.' The Normans rode out in three groups. The first contingent of twenty knights, the second of thirty knights, and the last of forty knights led by FitzGerald and Strongbow. They were supported by other less well-armed horsemen, archers, and some of the Norse-Irish townsmen. The Normans charged upon the retainers of Rory O'Connor, hoping to discourage the rest of his army. Rory was surprised, and as his men collapsed before the Normans, he escaped just in time to lead the Irish retreat.

From Dublin, Strongbow rode to Wexford. It was too late. Thinking that

Line drawing of a warrior from a miniature in the Dialogues of Saint Gregory, from a manuscript in the National Library of France, Paris. The coat of mail and nasal helmet was an international style of war-gear worn by almost all European knights of the eleventh century, including Celts.

Dublin had fallen to the Irish, FitzStephen had agreed to sail back to England. As his retainers gave up their arms, the men of Wexford threw FitzStephen into their dungeon and threatened to cut his head off if Strongbow should advance against them. Receiving a summons from his king, Strongbow returned to Britain. In south Wales, he reaffirmed his loyalty to Henry II and agreed to give up the conquered towns of Ireland in return for keeping Leinster as a fief. From a Welsh-Norman adventure, the assault on Gaelic Ireland had now developed into an Anglo-Norman invasion headed by the king of England.

Landing at Waterford with 500 knights and many more archers and light horsemen, Henry was greeted by the men of Wexford. Hoping to curry favour with the king, they offered him FitzStephen so he could be punished for invading Ireland without royal licence. This Henry did and FitzStephen was kept in chains as a royal prisoner until it was felt safe to pardon him. Henry paraded throughout Leinster. The lords of Cork, Limerick and many other southern Irish estates all did homage to him. They gave him hostages and agreed to pay a yearly tribute. At Dublin, Henry received the submission of Rory O'Connor and all the northern Irish lords except those of Ulster. He then convoked a synod of all the clergy of Ireland and tried to bring them in line with the English church. It seemed that the conquest of Ireland had been achieved with ease and only trouble at home forced Henry back to England. He was not to return to Ireland.

The submission of Rory O'Connor, lord of Connacht and high king of all Ireland, though attested by Giraldus, is not recorded by any other chronicler. With Henry gone and only Dublin and Leinster ruled by his governors, the north and west of Ireland remained Gaelic. Strongbow reasserted his hold over Leinster and led an attack against Munster. His first raid was successful, but his second met with complete defeat and he was pushed back to Waterford. Rory O'Connor led a force across the Shannon and ravaged the Normans in Meath. Strongbow struck back and by 1175 Meath was under Norman control. It was then that O'Connor made a formal submission to Henry II. It was acknowledged that Dublin, Meath and Leinster were to be ruled directly by the Normans, while the other Irish lords could rule their own lands in return for a yearly tribute of one hide for every ten animals slain. O'Connor remained Irish overlord. A year later, Strongbow was dead. His lands were held by the king and then divided among trusted vassals.

According to Giraldus, it would seem that the Celts of Ireland had been dealt a profound blow. Behind a rough diagonal from Cork and southern Munster to the eastern coast of Ulster, the Normans ruled from their stone-built castles. But how did the Irish see this invasion? Throughout the period described by Giraldus, the *Annals of Ulster* are very much concerned with the wars of the Celtic clans. The Normans—called Saxons in the *Annals*—are hardly mentioned and only then as a minor back-up force to Dermot MacMurrough: sometimes successful, sometimes not. 'They inflicted

In 1169, 30 Norman knights, 60 men-at-arms, and 300 archers landed at Bannow Bay in Leinster. A drawing by Alphonse de Neuville for Guizot's *L'Histoire de France*, 1870.

slaughter upon the Vikings of Dublin and Waterford and, on the other hand, many slaughters were inflicted upon themselves.' But, all the time, it is the Irish who are in control: conducting their own politics, their own wars. The only occasion the English are seen as a superior force is when King Henry lands with 240 ships. The Irish do homage to him, but the king soon leaves and the Irish lords continue their feuding. In the *Annals of Ulster*, the English—on the few occasions they are considered worthy of mention—are quickly absorbed into the Celtic world of raid and counter-raid.

To encounter such a perspective of the Normans in Ireland after reading that of Giraldus, encourages the view that Giraldus was engaged in the business of legend-making. His chronicle of the Normans in Ireland is a saga full of bold personalities and daring exploits. We are shown the Norman

84

invasion from the point of view of a handful of conquistadors, cutting their way into virgin territory held only by easily outwitted natives. Of course, this is how the English wished to view their first assault on the Irish. To them it was a heroic tale. Little did they realise, however, that the Irish considered the 'invasion' little more than a pinprick. The power-play of the Irish warlords remained, with the Normans now playing that role of opportunist auxiliaries formerly fulfilled by the Vikings. In time, both the Vikings and Normans were to be absorbed in the Irish way of war. Against the English, the North Men may have gained significant victories, but against Celtic warriors it had been a far longer, harder struggle: with no victors.

Celtic Counter-attack

WELSH
AND SCOTS
AGAINST THE
EDWARDIAN
KINGS
1200–1450

'To his most excellent lord, Philip, the illustrious king of the French . . .'. Llywelyn, lord of north Wales, supervised the composition of a letter of alliance. 'How am I to repay the excellence of your nobility,' the scribes continued, 'for the singular honour and priceless gift of sending me your knight with letter sealed in gold in testimony of the treaty between the kingdom of the French and the principality of north Wales. This letter I will keep in the church as if it were a sacred relic. An inviolable witness that I and my heirs will be friends to your friends and enemies to your enemies.'

There was more: the demand. 'Having summoned the council of my chief men and having obtained the common assent of all the princes of Wales, I promise that I will be faithful to you for ever. From the time I received your highness's letter, I have made neither truce nor peace with the English. By God's Grace, I and all the princes of Wales have manfully resisted our, and your, enemies. With God's Help we have by force of arms recovered from their tyranny a large part of the land and strong defended castles which by fraud they have occupied. Therefore, all the princes of Wales request that you make no truce with the English without us, knowing that we will not for any terms bind ourselves to them without your approval.'

When Llywelyn ab Iorwerth sent this treaty of alliance to the King of France in 1212, Celtic Wales was in a far stronger position than it had ever been since the Normans first surged into their land. In the previous century, the Welsh had made the most of crises in the English monarchy: the civil war of Stephen's reign; the unpopularity following Henry II's assassination of Thomas à Becket; the absence of Richard I on crusade in the Holy Land. Re-establishing themselves, the Welsh also adopted the castle-building of the Normans.

By the early thirteenth century, Llywelyn ab Iorwerth—Llywelyn the Great—had built a string of castles around Gwynedd. At Dolbadarn, dominating the mountain pass to Conwy, is a fully developed, strongly-fortified round stone keep, the match of any fortress built by the Marcher lords. In the heartland of the mountains of central Wales, stands Castell-y-Bere. Founded in 1221, the castle follows the shape of its base rock. Towers command each angle with the entrance protected by another tower and ditches cut in the rock. The towers are of the D-shaped type characteristic of Welsh castle-building. One served as the keep, while another was decorated with sculpture and probably contained a chapel. The high standard of stonework suggests this was one of Llywelyn's principal strongholds.

It was at the age of 21 in 1194 that Llywelyn claimed the throne of Gwynedd. He married the daughter of King John of England and gained a useful insight to the English way of power. He observed that a greater degree of centralisation was important to the maintenance of strength. Subsequently he cut across the native rivalry of the Welsh clans. Improvements in administration were coupled with the annexation of neighbouring Welsh estates. He did not lack for enemies among his own people. But, when King John set about cutting him down to size, it was Llywelyn's strength that encouraged the other Celtic warlords to join in his successful defence of Gwynedd. By 1215, baronial discord had undermined John's plans for Wales and the *Magna Carta* recognised that Celtic Wales, the Marches and English land in Wales were each ruled independently by the law of their own lords. Following hard on this victory, Llywelyn rode into south Wales at the head of a powerful array of united Welsh chieftains, leaving the English with few remaining footholds. Llywelyn was now overlord of Wales. He never actually called himself Prince of Wales, but preferred to honour himself as Prince of Aberffraw and Lord of Snowdon, to whom all other Welsh lords did homage. Even the Marcher lords were cowed.

Aside from their political strength, the Welsh were notably hardy fighters. 'In a certain part of this island, there is a people called the Welsh,' wrote King Henry II to the Emperor of Constantinople. 'They are so bold and so ferocious that even when unarmed, they do not fear to confront an armed force. Ready to shed their blood in defence of their country and to sacrifice their lives for renown. Even when the beasts of that land became calmed, these desperate men remained untamed.' Such hyperbole was probably intended as an excuse for Henry's lack of military success against the Welsh. But it is supported by Giraldus Cambrensis' description of their fighting spirit. 'The English fight in order to expel the natural inhabitants from the island and secure it all for themselves. The Welsh, who have for so

Drawing of a Welsh archer from the famous Register, Liber 'A', which includes the text of the Treaty of Montgomery, 1267, agreed between Llywelyn ap Gruffydd and Henry III. Correctly, the archer does not carry a 'longbow', supposedly characteristic of the Welsh, but an ordinary wooden bow probably more suited to the close-range archery praised by Giraldus Cambrensis.

long been sovereign over their land, maintain the conflict so that they may at least find a hiding place in the worst corner of it, among woods and marshes. The English fight for power, the Welsh for liberty. The English fight for money, the Welsh for their country.'

The Welsh warlords and their retainers were armed very much like their Norman-English enemies. They were mail-clad horse-warriors wielding sword and lance. It was their foot-soldiers, however, the common tribesmen, who seem to have contributed a particular Welshness to border warfare. 'The men of Gwent,' remarked Giraldus, 'are more used to war, more famous for their courage, and more expert in archery, than those of any other part of Wales. In an assault on the castle of Abergavenny, for example, two knights were passing over a bridge to take refuge in a tower built on a mound of earth. The Welsh, taking them in the rear, fired arrows that penetrated the oak door of the tower to a depth of four fingers. In memory of that feat, the arrows were preserved in the gate. William de Braose also testifies that one of his warriors was wounded by a Welsh arrow which passed through his mail clad thigh, his saddle, and penetrated his horse. Another knight had his armoured hip pierced by an arrow to the saddle. When he turned round, he received another arrow through his leg which fixed him to his horse. Yet the bows used by the Welsh are not made of horn, ivory, or yew, but of wild elm. They are unpolished and rough, yet stout. They are not intended to shoot an arrow at a great distance, but to inflict severe wounds in close fighting.'

It is generally assumed that it was amongst these talented Welsh archers that the celebrated longbow developed. In truth, there was no such weapon as the 'longbow' in the middle ages. It was referred to only as a 'bow', and the simple wooden bow used by the Welsh was common throughout Europe. What is significant, however, is that the English were so impressed by the forceful use of the bow by Welsh woodsmen, that they rapidly learned to employ large contingents of Welsh archers in their battles against the Irish, the Scots and each other. It was this deployment of large bodies of archers on the battlefield that was novel for the period. From this, of course, derived the tradition of massed Anglo-Welsh bowmen set against cavalry, culminating in the legendary archery triumphs of the Hundred Years War. What is surprising is that according to Giraldus the Welsh did not use their bows as the English were to—as a long-range shock weapon against organised formations of horsemen or foot-soldiers—but employed it as a precise close-range weapon in their guerilla wars of ambush.

Llywelyn ap Gruffyd maintained the strong, independent Wales that his grandfather, Llywelyn the Great, had built up. He exploited English weakness. The civil war between Henry III and his barons encouraged Llywelyn, under the guise of supporting Simon de Montfort, to attack the royalist Marcher lords. In 1265, this opportunism was transformed into a formal alliance. Simon recognised Llywelyn as Prince of Wales. Later that year, the wheel of fortune revolved, and Simon was killed at the battle of

Evesham by King Henry's son, Edward. In the fighting, the defeated Welsh auxiliaries of Simon were treated ruthlessly. They fled to a church for sanctuary. Undaunted, Edward and his warriors set about slaughtering the Welshmen, both inside and outside the church. Llywelyn now stood alone against the royalists, but his power was such that the war could only be brought to an end by treaty. In 1267, Henry III signed the Treaty of Montgomery, confirming Llywelyn as Prince of Wales and giving him the homage of all other Welsh chieftains. Llywelyn ap Gruffyd was riding high.

With King Henry's death in 1272, Edward claimed the throne. He was to be a formidable, unforgiving monarch. Llywelyn misjudged his character and immediately relations between the two warriors broke down. Although Edward's overlordship was never in doubt, Llywelyn nevertheless refused to attend the king's coronation. He refused to pay tribute and he refused to do homage. It now seemed as if Wales might break away completely as a separate state. In 1273, Edward sent a letter to Llywelyn, forbidding him to build a castle at Abermule near Montgomery. 'We have received a letter written in the king's name,' replied Llywelyn ironically. 'It forbids us to build a castle on our own land. We are sure it was not written with your

Welsh warrior with spear and sword, also illustrated in the Liber 'A' manuscript now in the Public Record Office, London. Alongside Welsh archers, Giraldus noted the fighting skill of the spearmen from north Wales. It has been suggested the one foot left naked was to enable a better grip on soggy terrain.

knowledge and would not have been sent if you had been in the country, for you know well that the rights of our principality are totally separate from the rights of your kingdom. We and our ancestors have long had the power within our boundaries to build castles without prohibition by any one.' Today the walls of Dorforwyn castle near Abermule still stand.

Edward harboured Llywelyn's disrespect until he was secure in his new crown. As for Llywelyn, it was not wholly his proud independence that repeatedly prevented him from paying homage. Many of Llywelyn's fiercest Welsh enemies had fled to the English court and the Welsh prince would be risking his life to ignore their presence. In 1276, Edward's patience snapped. He was an exceptionally able warlord and personally commanded all his armies. For the first two years of his reign he had fought in the Holy Land and defeated the Saracens at Haifa. For his first royal campaign on British soil, he assembled a powerful army of his own retainers and those of the Marcher lords. Overawed by Llywelyn, the Marcher lords were keen to reinstate their power. They spear-headed the invasion with two strikes against central Wales. In 1277, Edward took the field and advanced into northern Wales.

Llywelyn was unused to such English unity. He believed they were still divided by the split loyalties of the Barons' War. Instead, it was the Welsh who cracked up. Llywelyn's former Welsh allies broke away and marched alongside the English. Unprepared for such a rapid collapse of his power structure, there was little the Welsh prince could do. Literally cutting a path through the Welsh forests, Edward rode through the north of Wales, initiating the construction of a castle wherever he camped. Employing ships from the Cinque Ports, Edward cut off Llywelyn's supply lines from the grain-rich island of Anglesey. With only his faithful men of Gwynedd to protect him, Llywelyn was forced through hunger and the sheer size of Edward's campaign to admit a humiliating defeat. Llywelyn now not only paid homage to Edward, but lost much of the land he had conquered over the previous years. He lost also the homage of all his former Welsh vassals. He remained Prince of Wales, but this was now a meaningless title.

Retreating to his mountain castles, Llywelyn waited for events to overtake him. The English victory bit deep, and in 1282 it was Llywelyn's brother David who expressed Welsh resentment. Llywelyn had learned his lesson and repeated his homage to Edward, but, seeing his brother burn and loot English settlements, vengeance overcame caution. The rapidity of the uprising surprised Edward. Throughout Wales, Celtic warlords joined in an assault on the castles of the Marcher lords. Edward felt he had been generous in the first conflict, allowing the Welsh chieftains to keep their lands. Now he resolved to crush them. Gathering an army of feudal retainers and paid companies of crossbowmen and archers, he repeated his many-pronged campaign. Loyal Marcher lords rode into southern and central Wales, while the king's major force advanced from Chester. Edward again utilised ships to capture Anglesey. But this time, rather than waiting to starve out Llywelyn, one of his vassals, Luke de Tany, constructed a pontoon bridge across the Menai Strait to Bangor. Thus, Edward hoped to draw the net tight on Llywelyn and his followers in the mountains of Snowdon.

Carefully and efficiently, Edward captured castles on the mainland. But Luke was impatient. His warriors charged over the bridge. Ambushed by the Welsh, they rushed back to Anglesey. In the panic many were drowned. This victory temporarily bolstered the Welsh, who believed it a sign that, according to the prophecy of the legendary Merlin, Llywelyn would soon receive the crown of the Britons. The Welsh prince left his mountain lair to David and rode south. In a skirmish near Orewin bridge where the river Yrfor joins the Wye, he was confonted by the Marcher lord Roger Lestrange. Archers pelted the Welsh and then the mail-clad knights charged. In the fighting, Llywelyn was run through. His head was cut off and sent to Edward in north Wales. He in turn sent it to his warriors in Anglesey and then had it conveyed to London where it was stuck upon a spear and displayed at the Tower of London.

The Welsh were shattered. His own countrymen handed David over to the English. Wales was now under direct English control for the first time in its history. The Celtic heartland of Gwynedd became English crown lands. Edward's son, born at Caernarfon, was proclaimed Prince of Wales. A crown supposedly belonging to the legendary King Arthur was fortuitously uncovered and presented to Edward. He had become King of the Britons. This meant much to Edward: the Anglo-Normans had adopted Arthur as the leading hero of their cycle of chivalric tales. For had not Arthur defeated Saxons, just as the Normans had done? The Celts were furious that their national hero had been taken up by their enemies. Welsh propaganda maintained that Arthur was still alive in the mountains of Wales, awaiting his time to triumph over the enemies of his people. The English responded by uncovering the bones of the dead Arthur on English soil at Glastonbury. During his fighting in Wales, Edward deemed it important to interrupt his campaign to witness the disinterring of what were believed to be Arthur's bones and their reburial in a grander English tomb. Not only had the English taken the land of the Celts, they had stolen their legends.

The collapse of Celtic Wales cannot be wholly blamed on Llywelyn's over-confidence. It was Welsh misfortune to choose a fight with one of England's most powerful and effective rulers. Like other medieval kings, Edward had problems to settle in France, but throughout his reign these were overruled by his determination to increase English influence in Britain. Such a focus of attention, backed up by high military expertise, was bad news for the island's Celtic realms. For, after Wales, Edward set his sights on Scotland. In 1286, Alexander III, king of the Scots, went for a midnight ramble. 'Neither storm nor floods nor rocky cliffs, would prevent him from visiting matrons and nuns, virgins and widows, by day or by night as the fancy seized him.' On one of these adventures, Alexander

Gruffydd, son of Llywelyn the Great and father of Llywelyn the Last, tries to escape from the Tower of London. The rope snaps and he breaks his neck. After a drawing by Matthew Paris in his *Chronica Majora* of the thirteenth century in Corpus Christi College, Cambridge.

plunged over a cliff and was found with a broken neck. His only direct heir was his grand-daughter. Edward proposed a marriage between her and his son, the Prince of Wales. But she too met an untimely death. The competition for the Scots throne was now flung wide open.

Acknowledging his feudal and military superiority, the Scots regents allowed Edward to decide who should rule Scotland. The front runners were John Balliol and Robert the Bruce the Elder. Both these lords were descendants of the knights of William the Conqueror. For, by this time, Scotland, especially the lowlands, was dominated by Anglo-Norman landowners ruling estates throughout the realm. John Balliol ran vast estates in France; Robert the Bruce the Younger owned land in Essex. This conquest of Celtic Scotland had been achieved through court politics, intermarriage, and peaceful settlement. In the north, there were some Scots landowners and clansmen who were of direct Celtic descent, but increasingly the politics of the day was handled by warlords of Norman blood. The ensuing Anglo-Scots war can therefore be more clearly seen as a power struggle between Anglo-Norman dynasties and not an international war of Scots versus English or Celts against Normans, as was more true in Wales and Ireland. That said, the common people of Scotland and many of the lower aristocracy, the clansmen, were Celtic and still spoke Gaelic. It was these people, rallying to the cause of their Scots Norman masters, who may have envisaged their battle against the English invader as a national or Celtic struggle for independence.

Edward wanted to dominate Scotland. If he could not become its king, then he would choose the most malleable contender. He selected John Balliol as his puppet monarch. The elderly Robert the Bruce passed his family's claim onto his son, also called Robert the Bruce. They refused to do homage to the new king. Tiring of his humiliating role as frontman for Edward's ambitions, John Balliol renounced his allegiance to the English king and prepared for war. Robert the Bruce ignored his call to arms. Loyal to king Edward, it seemed now that Balliol might be displaced in favour of the Bruce claim.

Although embroiled in war in France and Wales, king Edward rode north with an army of English knights and Welsh archers. It may, incidentally, be thought remarkable that the Welsh should form such a major part of Edward's army so soon after their own defeat at his hands. But the defeat was against the Welsh Celtic nobility, whereas the ordinary Welshman was happy to fight for money and food on any side. For many of the Celtic nobility, however, Wales had ceased to be their homeland and several served abroad as mercenaries. Froissart, for instance, mentions an Owen of Wales who offered his services to the King of France during the Hundred Years War.

Berwick at once fell to Edward. His lieutenant, John de Warenne, shattered the Scots at Dunbar. Parading in triumph through Scotland, Edward demanded the abdication of Balliol. At Montrose, the two kings confronted each other. In front of both English and Scots courtiers, Balliol's coat of arms was ripped from him and thrown on the floor. His humiliation was complete. But Edward's arrogance had further heights to reach. Through fear alone, he received the homage of the Scots magnates. At Perth, he commanded that the sacred stone of Scone—upon which generations of Scots kings had been crowned—be removed and delivered to Westminster Abbey. Ignoring the Bruce claim, Edward appointed an English viceroy over the Scots. Scotland it seemed was now part of an English Empire. As Edward returned over the border, a chronicler recorded his concluding remarks on the campaign: 'It is a good job to be shot of shit.'

Recovering from Edward's blitzkrieg, a few Scots warlords set about reclaiming their dignity. Foremost among these was the Gaelic-speaking William Wallace. A man of low status and called by some a bandit, it may have been that Wallace was used by more powerful Scots aristocrats as a cover for their rebellion so they would be seen not to break their feudal vows of homage to Edward. In the *Lanercost Chronicle*, Wallace is called 'Willelmus Wallensis'—Welsh William—perhaps a reference to his Celtic tongue or his descent from the Britons of Strathclyde. Harassed by English tax collectors and hiding in the forest of Selkirk, Wallace gathered around him a band of outlaw warriors. One evening, he made a dash to see his lover. Surprised by an English patrol, he retreated into his woman's house and disappeared out the back door. The frustrated Englishmen set fire to the house and slaughtered Wallace's lover and family. The tall, angry Scotsman vowed vengeance. He had little time to wait. He and his retainers caught up with the English patrol and cut them to pieces.

This blow against the English encouraged several Scots aristocrats to raise their banners in rebellion. Among them were Sir William Douglas, the former commander of Berwick, and James Stewart, a major Scots land-owner. King Edward hoped to settle the insurrection with his Scots allies and sent Robert Bruce from his base in Carlisle to capture the Douglas castle. But Robert was none too sure of the righteousness of his order. His mother was Celtic and his deep feelings for the country of Scotland ran contrary to his family's political friendship. Besides, the Bruces had been used before with the promise of kingship and Edward had failed to deliver. At the castle of Douglas, Robert made the vital decision. He would fight with his countrymen, not against them.

In the meanwhile, William Wallace fought in the name of the deposed king, John Balliol. He readied his followers for a decisive clash with the English invaders. Committed to continental politics in 1297, king Edward sent John de Warenne to sort out the Scots. Wallace positioned his men in the hills around a bridge crossing the river Forth north of Sterling. Not all the Scots felt confident about the confrontation. James Stewart approached the English warlord with an offer of peace. Warenne refused and his knights began to advance across the bridge. With half the English over the river, it was then that Wallace pounced. Half his warriors fell upon the

94

leading English, while the rest set about chopping down the bridge. The English knights across the bridge floundered in the waterlogged fields of the river-bank. Scots spearmen pierced and prodded them off their horses. Scots axes rent the rings of English mail. With the bridge destroyed, the English vanguard was isolated. Their comrades on the south side of the river could only watch as the Scots wiped out the beleaguered knights. Among the dead was Hugh de Cressingham, chief tax collector of Edward's

The mighty four-towered gatehouse of Harlech Castle. Built by Edward I between 1283 and 1290 to prevent Snowdonia from ever becoming a region of stiff Welsh resistance.

regime in Scotland. His body was flayed and Wallace had a broad strip of his skin from head to heel made into a baldric for his sword. John de Warenne and the rest of the English fled back to Berwick. James Stewart captured their baggage train on the way.

In the forest of Selkirk, William Wallace was proclaimed Guardian of the Kingdom of Scotland and knighted by Robert Bruce. The Earl of Carrick, Bruce had himself roused the men of his own estate and Galloway to the

Reconstruction of the seal of king Edward I, showing the scourge of the Celts in full knightly panoply.

96

common cause, but had yet to meet the English in battle. Throughout the rest of 1297, Wallace ravaged the border land of England for corn and cattle. Such a turn of events wrenched Edward back from his adventuring in Europe. He transferred his headquarters to York. Now he would hammer the Scots. Feudal dues were called upon. Gascon crossbowmen and Welsh archers were recruited. A vast supply train of wagons and ships was assembled. By the summer of 1298, 2,500 horse-warriors and 12,000 foot-soldiers marched into Scotland. The Scots retreated before the mighty army. But the further the English advanced, the more their supplies began to break down. Their ships brought no food, only wine. Fighting broke out between the Welsh and the English. With his expedition on the brink of collapse, Edward suddenly caught wind of the Scots. The action would take place on hills near Falkirk.

William Wallace feared the greater numbers of the English horsemen. To counter them, he positioned his spear-carrying foot-soldiers behind boggy land, with woodland and rough terrain guarding their flanks. The spears of the Scots were long pikes and they stood in crowded phalanx formations—schiltrons—presenting the enemy with a forest of iron points. In front of the spearmen, stakes were hammered into the ground with ropes joining them. Groups of archers gathered between the schiltrons. The few Scots horsemen waited in reserve, hoping to exploit any break in the enemy. King Edward realised his superiority in horse-warriors and sent his knights in on the first wave of the attack. Galloping into the marshland, the horses slowed down. The majority of the English horsemen then wheeled to the left and right and rode round the swamp, hitting the Scots in the rear.

The shock of battle scattered the Scots horsemen and the English now plunged amid their foot-soldiers. The bows of the Scots had little penetrating power against the mail of the English and soon they too had joined the routed horsemen. But the Scots spearmen held firm. Their rope and stake entanglements tripped up the English horses: knights crashed to the ground. The English men at arms could not break the relentless rows of pikes. The Master of the Templars rushed too recklessly on the spear forest, flailing madly with his sword, hoping to break it with his animal strength. He and his five retainers were impaled. By this time, Edward and his foot-soldiers had caught up with his knights and called off their rash attacks. With no enemy horse or archers to harry him, Edward gathered his Welsh bowmen in front of the Scots schiltrons. They fired hail after hail into the standing targets. The stalwart Scots could only take so much. Men fell and gaps appeared in the once formidable spear wall. It was then that Edward sent his knights in among the broken formations. With war hammer, mace and sword, the horse-warriors hacked at the Gaelic underlings. William Wallace escaped the slaughter, but his power perished with his army.

Edward's victory at Falkirk was not complete. The countryside remained hostile and he was desperately short of supplies, forcing him to retreat to the border. In Carlisle, he sent out summonses for warriors for yet further

campaigns. His obsession turned the lowlands into a devastated killing ground. Among the Scots, William Wallace returned to his raiding: there would be no key role for him. In 1305, he was betrayed by demoralised countrymen, dragged through the streets of London, half hanged and then dismembered. The next year, Robert Bruce eliminated his only serious rival to the Scots throne and had himself crowned Robert I. The English fell upon him with a vengeance. His retainers were smashed at the battle of Methven. Members of his family were executed. His lover and sister held like animals in cages on the battlements of Berwick and Roxburghe castles. Robert was reduced to the life of a fugitive, hunted by Scotsmen eager for the bounty placed on his head by Edward.

When Robert emerged from hiding in 1307, the harsh retribution of the English had provided Bruce with many fresh supporters. But his greatest break was yet to come. As the elderly king Edward prepared to launch another assault, the veteran warrior died. The aura of inevitable victory that seemed always to follow the English when led by Edward was at last at

Caernarfon Castle, begun in 1283 and built by Edward I to command the entrance of the Menai Strait. These castles are still regarded by many Welshmen as unacceptable symbols of English domination.

an end. But Edward's determination to subdue the Scots lived on. He had extracted from his son two promises: first, that the Prince of Wales should carry on the fight against Bruce; and, second, that Edward's coffin be carried ahead of his army into Scotland.

Edward II could not hope to be the supreme warlord his father had been. It was not until 1310 that this king of England crossed the border. In the meantime, Robert's guerilla warfare had undermined his enemies in Scotland and he had regained his leadership of the Scots. In 1308, it is said, he held a parliament at St Modan's Priory, Ardchattan, at which the business was conducted in Gaelic: perhaps an acknowledgement to the loyal support of the clansmen and the lower Scots classes. Eventually, Edward II did march against Bruce. But Robert avoided confrontation, devastated the land before him, and the English had to turn back. Robert now took the war across the border and ravaged Northumberland. In Scotland, he reduced resistant castles one by one, until only Sterling held out. The revival of Robert's power was remarkable. From a fugitive to chief Scots warlord in just over two years: a clear sign of his popular support.

In 1314, Edward II gathered a great army outside Berwick to raise the siege of Sterling: 500 knights accompanied by 2,000 mounted retainers;

Battle axe discovered in the Thames, thirteenth or fourteenth century, now in the London Museum. The breadth of the cutting edge is 17 cm (7 in).

3,000 Welsh archers and 15,000 foot-soldiers armed with spear, pole-axe, dagger and shield. In his eagerness to finish off Bruce, Edward marched his men into the ground. By the time they reached a little stream called Bannock, north of Falkirk, they were exhausted. It was then that Robert brought his men out of his lair in the forest of Torwood and confronted the English. His army was around a quarter of the numbers of Edward's. His warriors came from all over Scotland. His 5,000 massed spearmen consisted of lowlanders and highlanders, with some soldiers coming from the Western Isles. Bruce himself commanded a phalanx of Gaelic clans. These were led into battle by their own clan chieftains. The following claim to have been represented: Cameron, Campbell, Chisholm, Fraser, Gordon, Grant, Gunn, MacKay, MacIntosh, Macpherson, Macquarrie, Maclean, MacDonald, MacFarlane, MacGregor, MacKenzie, Menzies, Munro, Robertson, Ross, Sinclair and Sutherland. Among the bristling schiltrons, there were a few archers and about 500 lightly clad horsemen. This was the same battle formation that had been devastated at Falkirk.

Although short in numbers, Robert hoped to make up for this deficiency by training his men hard. The Scots knew how to wield their 12-foot spears, stand tight in their formations, and resist the temptation to run wildly into the conflict. Bruce prepared the ground around the burn of Bannock carefully. Pits were dug and then covered with brushwood. Tree trunks were built into barricades across forest paths. The time of combat was getting nearer. Robert dispatched his camp followers to a nearby valley.

On the morning of the battle, the Scots celebrated mass. By midday, the English had ridden into view. The first warriors on the field were the vanguard of English knights. They expected to overawe the Scots with their brilliant armour and streaming pennons. In the open ground between the two armies they came across a few Scots scouting out the land. Among them was Robert Bruce. One of the leading English knights, Sir Humphry de Bohun, recognized the Scots king, couched his lance, and spurred his horse into a gallop. Seeing the English knight powering towards him, the sensible reaction for Robert would have been to fall back. His death would mean the end of the battle. But to turn now, in front of his own men, would be equally disastrous. Besides, Robert had a particular loathing for the knight de Bohun. When he had been on the run, Edward I had handed his estates in Annandale and Carrick over to the de Bohuns. Later, Edward II gave the Bruce's estates in Essex to the same family. Robert urged his grey palfrey on towards the duel. Henry de Bohun's lance charge was deflected. Robert stood in his stirrups, raised his battleaxe high and brought it crashing down on the knight's helmet, splitting it and breaking open his head, shattering the axe shaft. A great cry went up from the highlanders. They clambered over their earthworks and ran on towards the English horsemen. Thrown into a panic by the hidden pits and charging Celts, the English backed off.

Elsewhere on the battlefield, another group of English knights rode upon the Scots. This time they were confronted by a schiltron of spearmen. Of the

The abbot of Inchaffray
blesses the Scots
highlanders of the
schiltron before the battle
of Bannockburn, 1314.
From Cassell's *Illustrated
Universal History*, 1884.

two leading English knights, one was killed immediately, the other
captured, his horse being impaled on the pikes. The rest rode more
cautiously around the circle of spears. Out of desperation, some threw their
knives, lances and maces at the Scots. The spearmen thrust at the horses.
Eventually, the intense summer heat proved decisive, and the humbled,
sweating Englishmen rode off. That night, the Scots were convinced they
had done enough to claim victory and were ready to decamp. Certainly,
across the battleground, panic had swept through the English ranks; so
much so that king Edward had to send heralds around his camp to assure
the men that the conflicts so far had been mere skirmishes, the main battle
was yet to come. In the meanwhile, English deserters reassured Robert of
his success and encouraged him to stay with the promise of an absolute
victory the next day.

During that short summer night, the English knights had taken the best
ground around Bannockburn for their brief rest. Their archers and foot-
soldiers had been forced to lie on the soggy, marshy land near the stream. In
the dawn light, the English knights impatiently mounted their horses, keen

to avenge the humiliation they had suffered the previous day. They expected Robert to remain in his defensive position, awaiting their attack. Instead, the Scots took the offensive, rolling down the hillside in three densely-packed schiltrons. Foot-soldiers daring to attack horsemen! The English could not believe their luck. The Earl of Gloucester was among the first of the knights to charge upon the Scots. Spears cracked and splintered, but the Scots held firm. No matter how many knights hurled themselves on the forest of points, the schiltrons rolled on.

With their knights already immersed in the fighting, the Welsh and English archers had little opportunity to break the Scots with their arrow storm. The battle was now a hand-to-hand struggle. Axe against sword. Spears thrust through visors. The lightly-armoured Scots leaped among the fallen mail-clad knights, hammering them mercilessly. The Scots crushed the English towards the marshy river bank. Despite the chaos of the crowded

Robert Bruce commanding his Highland warriors at the Battle of Bannockburn. After having routed an enemy, warriors of the schiltron would often jump on horses and thus drive home their victory. From Cassell's *History of England*, 1905.

fighting, English arrows still fell hard and these Robert feared most. He therefore ordered his small band of 500 horsemen forward against the archers, cutting them down. The schiltrons pressed on. Robert sent in his reserves. Scotsmen leaned on their comrades in front, pushing and heaving forward. English knights trampled their fellow warriors into the mud in desperation to escape. Horses and men fell into the stream, drowning. Realising the battle was over, English noblemen grabbed the reins of their king and led him away. With victory safe, the Scots camp followers, women and children, joined in the final struggle, looting and slaughtering. With their make-shift banners held high, it appeared to the English that a second Scots army had arrived and their rout was completed.

Bannockburn was a devastating defeat for the English. The Earl of Gloucester, thirty-four barons, and two hundred knights were among the dead. Nearly a hundred other knights had been captured, to be ransomed over the next year. Robert Bruce was undisputed king of Scotland. In the aftermath, the Scots paid back the English for all those years of invasion. They swept south and raided northern England as far as Durham and Richmond in Yorkshire. They drove back herds of cattle and wagons of loot. The English dared not confront the Scots and Northumberland was left to fend for itself. But the victory of Bannockburn also allowed Robert to consider a grander strategy. He sent his brother, Edward, to Ireland. Some said this was merely an excuse to rid Scotland of a strong rival to Robert's throne, providing Edward with the chance to win a crown of his own. However, it also made good strategic sense. The English estates in Ireland had been a source of warriors and supplies for the armies of both Edward I and Edward II. It was also part of a general Scots determination to master the Irish Sea. For, as soon as Edward had landed in Ireland, his fleet was returned to Robert who used it to secure the homage of the Norse-Scots lords of the Western Isles.

In Ireland, Robert Bruce hoped to arouse a sense of Celtic brotherhood. He sent before Edward a remarkable letter addressed to all the Irish chieftains. 'We and our people and you and your people,' he proclaimed, 'free since ancient times, share the same national ancestry and are urged to come together more eagerly and joyfully in friendship by a common language and by common custom. We have sent to you our beloved kinsman, the bearer of this letter, to negotiate with you in our name about permanently maintaining and strengthening the special friendship between us and you, so that with God's will your nation may be able to recover her ancient liberty.' Clearly, the medieval Scots were aware of their Irish ancestry and now wished to call upon that valued Gaelic aspect of their nationhood to overthrow the Norman-Saxon English. In the wake of Bannockburn, the Irish were indeed tempted by the successful independence of the Scots. The O'Neills of Ulster were particularly keen to hit back at the English and offered Edward Bruce their kingship.

Donal O'Neill called upon fellow Irishmen to support Edward against the 'sacrilegious and accursed English who, worse than the inhuman Danes, are busy heaping injuries of every kind upon the inhabitants of this country.' He noted that their past disunity had made the Irish vulnerable: 'we, being weakened by wounding one another, have easily yielded ourselves a prey to them. Hence it is that we owe to ourselves the miseries with which we are afflicted, manifestly unworthy of our ancestors, by whose valour and splendid deeds the Irish race in all past ages has retained its liberty.'

Landing at Lough Larne in Ulster, Edward Bruce led an army of 6,000. A small force, it nevertheless comprised veteran warriors of the war of independence and soon defeated the local Anglo-Irish barons. A few Irish chieftains immediately allied themselves with Bruce, but others had to be beaten into submission. Despite a call for Celtic unity, this would become a campaign as much against the native Irish as against the English. The Scots' progress through the country sent out ripples of mayhem. An army from Connacht arose to confront him, but was split by Edward playing off one clan against another so that Connacht was itself plunged into civil war. In 1316, in Dundalk, Edward Bruce was crowned High King of all Ireland. He now invited his brother to survey his newly conquered territory. Robert Bruce arrived with a powerful force of galloglas, notoriously ferocious Norse Gaelic mercenaries from the Hebrides. So far, Robert's masterplan had worked well. With Edward in Ireland, the Western Isles under Robert's control, rumours soon spread that the Bruces were to land in Wales and restore their ancient liberty. An all-Celtic movement seemed imminent, unifying the Celts against Edwardian England. Encouraged by such thoughts, the Welsh rose in revolt under Llywelyn Bren. Edward II could not even trust his Welsh archers and all ideas of a counter-attack against Scotland had to be forgotten as he defended his lands in Wales and Ireland.

In Ireland, it was customary that a High King parade all round the country to secure his homage and respect. Early in 1317, Edward Bruce set out with his brother on just such an expedition. They received a rough welcome. The earl of Ulster set an ambush. Allowing Edward's vanguard to proceed through forestland, he then set his archers on Robert's rear. Robert was not provoked and maintained his warriors in good order—except for his nephew Sir Colin Campbell: he spurred his horse on towards the Irish despite the likelihood of a trap. Robert dashed after him and stunned him with a blunt weapon before he could be surrounded. At that moment, more warriors emerged from the forest and a fierce struggle ensued. Only the discipline and military expertise of the Scots saved them from the superior numbers of the Irish.

The people of Dublin, fearing that Edward would march on them next, demolished and set fire to the suburban buildings outside their walls so as to deprive the Scot's army of any cover. It was a decision they were later to regret, for they destroyed many important buildings in their panic, including the king of England's Irish manor. And, anyway, Edward had little time for a siege and had decided to bypass the stout defences of the

Robert Bruce kills the English knight Sir Humphry Bohun with a single blow in the first day of the battle of Bannockburn. From Cassell's *British Battles on Land and Sea*.

city. The Bruces advanced into Munster, for here Irish clansmen promised that the entire countryside would rise to their side. But mutual suspicions overrode these ambitious plans and famine prevented any successful campaigning. Edward was forced to turn back and consolidate his base in Ulster. After such an anti-climax, Robert returned to Scotland. The shockwaves of Bannockburn had begun to recede and Edward II was able to act with more confidence in the support of his barons. A small force of Genoese crossbowmen was sent to Ireland to encourage the cause of the English. Through a generous attitude to enemies and a consolidation of feudal privileges, king Edward managed to increase his influence among the Anglo-Irish. A royal mission to the Pope had also brought benefits. Archiepiscopal vacancies in Ireland were filled by men favourable to king Edward and all supporters of both Bruces were excommunicated. It appeared that Edward II was far more astute at politics than warfare.

Donal O'Neill, self-styled king of Ulster and 'true heir by hereditary right of all Ireland', wrote to Pope John XXII with the Irish point of view. He detailed how the English dominated his land and treated the Irish as inferior

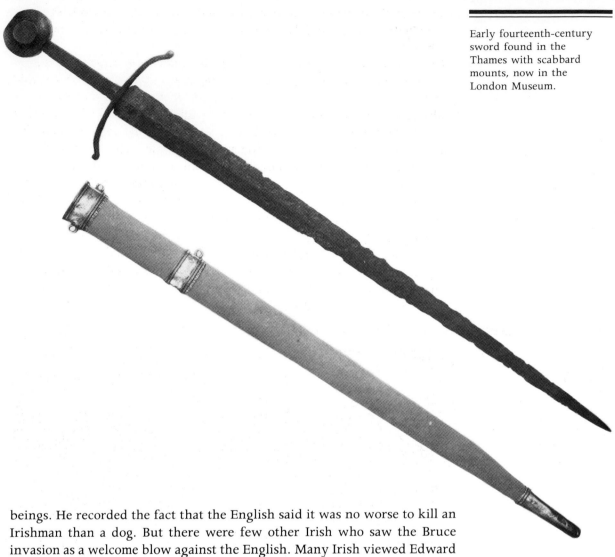

Early fourteenth-century sword found in the Thames with scabbard mounts, now in the London Museum.

beings. He recorded the fact that the English said it was no worse to kill an Irishman than a dog. But there were few other Irish who saw the Bruce invasion as a welcome blow against the English. Many Irish viewed Edward as yet another alien adventurer and preferred to do business with the English simply because they had been longer established. A chronicler of Connacht summed up Bruce's army as: 'Scottish foreigners less noble than our own foreigners.' As for the ideal that both Irish and Scots should unite under a common Gaelic banner, this seems to have been soon forgotten by both sides in the powerplay that followed invasion. Among the remote tribesmen of the Irish mountains who did join Edward Bruce, the prospect may have appealed of fighting alongside warriors speaking a similar Celtic language. But, by 1318, Edward Bruce still only had the support of a few Ulster opportunists. The action of English privateers in the Irish Sea had broken the dominance of the Scots and reinforcements from Scotland could not be depended on. Nevertheless, Edward Bruce was a potent political force and, supported by the de Lacy family, he rode southwards at the head of an Irish-Scots army over two thousand strong. An Anglo-Irish force under Richard Clare, Lord Lieutenant of Ireland, met him at Faughart, just north of Dundalk.

Bruce was heavily outnumbered and his senior knights advised him to wait for reinforcements. But Bruce was impatient for a victory that would give him greater political control. His Irish allies refused to join in the foolhardiness and suggested they harry the English with raids while Bruce awaited the extra men that were expected. Again Edward ignored this sound advice and sent his warriors into battle. The vanguard and mainguard became spread out, their thin numbers annihilated piecemeal by the Anglo-Irish. Loyal to death, Edward's knightly retainers charged alongside their leader as the rearguard rumbled forward. Having belated thoughts of mortality, Edward exchanged his conspicuous royal armour for the plainer garb of a lowly knight. The Scots fought bravely, but inevitably were overwhelmed. According to legend, the English found the body of the lowly knight clad in royal armour and presumed it to be Edward Bruce. His head was cut off, salted in a bucket, and sent to Edward II. But the Bruce

Section of early fourteenth-century mail. By this period, plate armour had become more important and the ubiquitous mail coat shortened.

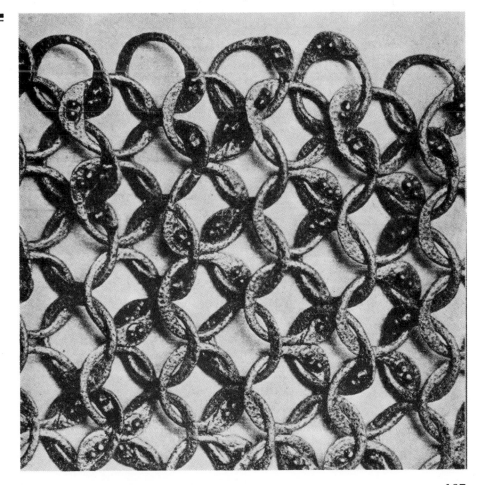

had not escaped the slaughter. His body lay elsewhere on the battlefield. As the Gaelic prisoners were led away, a Scots knight Sir Philip Mowbray regained consciousness and broke away with other captives. They carried the heavy news of Edward Bruce's death to Scotland.

In that second decade of the fourteenth century, it seemed as if the Celtic realms of Britain and Ireland might rise together and throw back the descendants of the Normans and Saxons. In the event such a dream did not come true, and the English held onto many of their Celtic possessions. But the struggle had not been in vain. In Ireland, English control had been further weakened. Irish chieftains contested the land as strongly as the Anglo-Irish barons. Although some admitted the overlordship of the English king, all were united in their determination not to be ruled by a middle strata of Anglo-Irish adventurers.

Norman dynasties were bundled out of several Irish estates. A Gaelic revival was under way that would eventually reduce the power of the English to the Pale—the royal territory around Dublin. The authority of the great Irish lordships emerged intact from the Celtic highlands. Already, in 1258, an attempt had been made to restore the high kingship of all Ireland. In 1327, Leinster—the heartland of Anglo-Irish support—had thrown itself behind the MacMurroughs and elected one of them king of Leinster, the first since the Norman conquest. Military victories were paralleled by a resurgence of Gaelic culture that engulfed the Anglo-Irish and ensured that the Celtic tongue and law were dominant in Ireland until the coming of the Tudors.

In Scotland, the struggle had been decisive. The Scots had powerfully secured their border. No Englishman dared set foot on Scots land in the years following Bannockburn. In battle, Gaelic-speaking, spear-wielding common foot-soldiers had shown they were the equal of any lance-carrying, knightly horse-warrior. Above all, the Scots had a king from their own country. Robert Bruce was an intelligent and ingenious warlord and repelled all attacks on his kingdom by Edward II until the unpopular English monarch was murdered in 1327. In 1328, the young Edward III acknowledged at last Robert's title of king and a 13-year truce was agreed. A year later the Bruce was dead. Hostilities recommenced, but a legend of Scots independence had been established.

In Wales, the mere rumour of a Bruce invasion had been enough to encourage the Welsh to rebel. Throughout the rest of the fourteenth century, the English managed to control the principality, but such Celtic anger could not be stemmed forever. When it burst in 1400, it was not in the form of a nationalist uprising; there were very few such movements in the Middle Ages. It broke as a feud between Marcher lords. That it then developed into a popular strike for independence is a tribute to the charisma of its leader: Owain Glyndwr. Here was a Welsh warlord who satisfied both the English and the Celtic qualifications of leadership. Descended from the royal family of Llywelyn, he could rightfully claim to be

Scots footsoldier armed with pike and sword as he might have fought in the famed schiltron. From the thirteenth-century Liber 'A' manuscript now in the Public Record Office, London.

Reconstruction of the seal of Robert Bruce, king of Scotland, now in the National Library of France, Paris.

109

Prince of North Wales. But he also satisfied the older Celtic tradition of a warrior accepted by his peers as chieftain because of his military prowess and because he was the most competent figure to fill the role.

Although of Welsh blood, Glyndwr was a perfect English knight. He fought loyally and bravely for the king of England against the Scots and was a respected member of the English court. In 1400, he was a middle-aged man when he returned to his family estate in north Wales. He probably considered himself to be in retirement. He was an unlikely hero of what was to follow. When a border dispute with his neighbour, Lord Grey of Ruthin, irritated him beyond endurance, he did not immediately take to arms, but chose to settle the argument through the English parliament. The mood at Westminster was far from sympathetic to the Welsh. A civil war had rent the kingdom. Henry IV had defeated Richard II. The Welsh had supported Richard's claim. Eager to demonstrate their loyalty to the new king, English lords were far from keen to support the cause of a Welshman. Owain's case was dismissed. He accepted the decision, but events would not leave him alone.

The siege of Carlisle by the Scots in 1315. Line drawing of the initial letter from the charter granted to the city by Edward II in recognition of their successful defence. The Scots' siege engines were not used to good effect in the assault.

Irish footsoldier of the time Edward Bruce landed in Ireland. A drawing from the Liber 'A' manuscript now in the Public Record Office, London.

Lord Grey, as chief Marcher lord, was entrusted by king Henry to raise warriors in north Wales for a campaign against the Scots. He sent notice to all the king's subjects, demanding their presence in the royal retinue. If subjects did not respond to this duty then their lands could be taken away from them, for they received them only on condition of their service to the king. Whether by chance or ploy, the summons to arms arrived too late at the estate of Owain for him to gather his forces and join the king. His absence was noticed, and in the ensuing defeat at the hands of the Scots a furious king empowered Lord Grey to arrest Glyndwr. According to tradition, Glyndwr escaped from the trap set by Grey and began raising forces against the Marcher chief. On the banks of the Dee at Carrog, he was crowned Prince of Wales. Bards spread it far and wide that the stream in which the decapitated head of Llywelyn the Last had been washed now ran with blood.

Glyndwr's followers struck back at Ruthin, Grey's town. They then raided Denbigh, Flint, Hawarden, Holt, Rhuddlan, Oswestry and Welshpool. Glyndwr was declared an outlaw and his estates confiscated. In turn, he set up a mountain stronghold in Snowdonia on the shores of Lake Peris. Support was growing for Glyndwr, but his immediate military power was undercut by royal pardons issued to all Welsh rebels apart from their leader. The Marcher lords required sterner measures to protect their interests. A state of emergency was declared which effectively took all power of administration and law away from native Welshmen and handed it over to the English. Even the Welsh students ensconced in English universities were outraged and there were skirmishes with the citizens of Oxford. The situation deteriorated into open warfare. In 1401, the Tudor brothers from Anglesey captured the castle at Conwy. A year later, the rumour that the deposed king Richard was still alive stiffened opposition to Henry IV.

Avoiding confrontation, Glyndwr's warriors spread the rebellion from the north of Wales to the south. In a mountain glen in the Hyddgen valley, near Llanidloes, Glyndwr's guerilla band of 400 men was surrounded by 1500 Flemish immigrants and merchants of south Wales, fiercely determined to protect their newly-established colonies. For Owain, it was death or surrender. But the Welsh rebels were hardened fighters and they savaged the Flemish civilians. It was Glyndwr's first victory in a pitched battle and it increased his following overnight. Such a force, however, could not hope to survive the mighty army that Henry IV now assembled to finish off the Welsh. In desperation, Glyndwr wrote to both the kings of Ireland and Scotland. 'So long as we shall wage manfully this war on our borders,' he told the Gaelic high king of Ireland, 'so you and all other chieftains of your parts of Ireland will in the meantime have welcome peace and quiet repose.' Unfortunately, both letters were intercepted by king Henry. There would be no union of the Celtic realms.

Henry's army burned and ransacked monasteries and villages. It took

111

Irishmen fighting with axes. After the illustrations in Giraldus Cambrensis' early thirteenth-century *Topographia Hibernica & Expugnatio Hiberniae*, now in the National Library of Ireland, Dublin.

prisoner the children of suspected rebels. But it came nowhere near to ending Welsh independence. Glyndwr emerged from his mountain lair to capture Lord Grey of Ruthin. By 1404, he was at the height of his power. He summoned a national Welsh parliament which all the leading Welsh magnates attended. His unity was greater even than that of Llywelyn, for Powys had always remained aloof: now Powys did homage to Glyndwr. He planned to establish a separate Welsh church and university. He made individual treaties with France and Scotland. It seemed that Welsh independence would again become reality.

In 1405, the French invaded Britain. Almost 3,000 French warriors landed at Milford Haven. They were met by an army of 10,000 Welshmen. Together they would smash the English. At Caerleon, the French marvelled at the Roman amphitheatre. They were told it was the original Round Table of the Arthurian knights and that, of course, Arthur was the warrior hero of the Celtic Britons and not the English. Worcester, the first major English town in their path, was devastated. At Woodbury Hill, they set up camp.

Kidney daggers, fourteenth to fifteenth centuries, now in the London Museum. Commonly a civilian weapon, but also carried by archers in battle.

They were confronted by an English army led by king Henry's son, the future Henry V. Apparently, with their minds full of Arthurian legend, the Franco-Welsh challenged the English not to battle but to a tournament. For eight days, knights of both sides hurtled towards each other with lance and sword. Two hundred died in the sporting combat. Eventually Prince Henry tired of the game. He retired to Worcester and then turned on the retreating French, harrying their rearguard. Some French sailed home, others stayed with the Welsh. The ambitious expedition had run out of steam and the tide now turned for Glyndwr.

From 1406 onwards, Prince Henry and the English tightened the ring around Glyndwr's principality. The Marches were won back slowly and the Welsh retreated to the mountains of central Wales. As always, the superior economic and logistical back-up of the English was beginning to dominate the struggle. But the Glyndwr was far from finished. In 1415, Henry V sent an envoy to offer a pardon to the Welshman. Owain refused. It was then that Glyndwr became swathed in legend. His whereabouts were unknown. The chronicles are silent. The date and site of his death are a mystery. Many Welshmen were convinced that like Arthur, Glyndwr was asleep in a cave in the heart of Wales awaiting the right time to lead his people to freedom. The inspiration of Celtic liberty remained. But increasingly, despite the action of heroic warlords, the future of all the Celtic realms of Britain and Ireland was haunted by the English. In the next century, Celtic warriors would face the final challenge to their independence. It came from a dynasty of Celtic ancestry: the Tudors.

The Final Challenge

For two hundred years, English influence in Ireland declined. From the invasion of Edward Bruce to the rise of the Tudor dynasty, the power of the English crown had been so reduced that in 1465 the Pale included only the four home counties of Dublin, Kildare, Meath and Louth: a frontier of not even 150 miles. Civil war and continental conflict had undermined English control, but it was also the independent Celtic spirit of the Irish warlords. The majority of Anglo-Irish lords, descendants of the Normans, had gone native. Their language, appearance and law was Gaelic. Militarily, the Irish were no longer cowed by English or Welsh mercenaries. They had fierce mercenaries of their own. Emerging from the ancient relationship between Ulster and the Scots Isles and Western Highlands, a potent military force had developed over the two centuries since Edward Bruce. Scots adventurers and families of professional warriors sailed to Ireland intent on hiring themselves out to the highest bidder. These were the galloglas, a fiery mixture of Scots, Irish and Norse.

Galloglas means 'foreign young warrior' and probably refers to their Viking blood. But, essentially, these warriors were Gaelic in tongue and custom. Some had accompanied Edward Bruce and many fought for the Ulster chieftains. As their notoriety grew, they were hired by other Irish warlords. Such business enabled generations of galloglas families to prosper from Gaelic feuds. The principal mercenary dynasties were the MacDonalds, MacSwineys, MacSheehys, MacDowells, MacRorys and MacCabes. It was only a matter of time before the English felt the need to

116

employ them as well. In between bouts of fighting, the galloglas set up their own settlements on Irish territory. By the sixteenth century they had become an institution and were the elite of every Irish army. John Dymmok in the late sixteenth century captured their basic image: 'The galloglas are picked and select men of great and mighty bodies, cruel without compassion. The greatest force of the battle consisteth in them, choosing rather to die than to yield, so that when it cometh to bandy blows, they are quickly slain or win the field.' Such a description of the short bursts of fighting energy of Celtic warriors could have come from the pens of Latin writers of the first centuries AD. Perhaps the English saw themselves as the new Romans and so inflicted such classical imagery on their Celtic opponents. 'They are armed with a shirt of mail, a skull [*close-fitting iron helmet*], and a skean [*long knife*],' continued Dymmok. 'The weapon which they most use is a battle-axe or halberd, six foot long, the blade whereof is somewhat like a shoemaker's knife, but broader and longer without pike [*that is, spike*], the stroke whereof is deadly where it lighteth. And being thus armed, reckoning to him a man for his harness bearer, and a boy to carry his provisions, he is named a spare [*spear? or 'sparre' meaning a long-handled axe*] of his weapon so called, 80 of which spares make a battle of galloglas.' Although frequently from noble families and regarded as gentlemen soldiers by the English, the galloglas did not fight on horseback, but assembled in bodies of heavily-armoured foot-soldiers.

On an equal ranking were Irish horse-warriors. 'Their horsemen are all gentlemen (I mean of great septs or names, how base soever otherwise),' noted Fynes Moryson in 1600 with a pertinent afterthought. Like the galloglas, many were professional soldiers of fortune. 'These horsemen,' wrote Rochard Stanihurst in 1577, 'when they have no stay of their own [*that is, are not retained by any lord*], gad and range from house to house like errant knights of the Round Table, and they never dismount until they ride into the hall and as far as the table.' They were highly respected as light cavalry by the English. Sir Anthony St Leger remarked on them in a letter to Henry VIII in 1543: 'I think for their feat of war, which is for light scourers, there are no properer horsemen in Christian ground, nor more hardy, nor yet that can better endure hardness.' Later in the century, Edmund Spenser concurred: 'I have heard some great warriors say that in all the services which they had seen abroad in foreign countries they never saw a more comely horseman than the Irishman, nor that cometh on more bravely in his charge.'

It seems the high skill of Celtic horsemanship had not deserted the Irish. And yet, in other descriptions of Irish cavalry we have a clear picture of a military primitivism that is supposed to have been characteristic of Irish warfare. 'The horsemen are armed with head-pieces, shirts of mail or jacks [*leather quilted coats sometimes plated with iron*], a sword, a skein, and a spear. They ride upon pads [*stuffed saddles*] or pillons without stirrups, and in this differ from ours; that in joining with the enemy, they bear not their

staves or lances under arm, and so put it to rest, but taking it by the middle, bear it above arm, and so encounter.' Contemporary engravings reinforce this image of stirrupless riders, while Edmund Spenser states that among the Irish 'the stirrup was called so in scorn as it were a stair to get up'. It is baffling that, alone among all Europe's horse-warriors, the Irish chose to ride without stirrups or good saddles. It seems more likely that such primitivism was an invention of the English to play up their barbarity. Yet it is mentioned and illustrated by several sources, not all of them wholly uncomplimentary to the Irish. There seems little point either to focus on this detail when the general character of the Irish was found sufficient by the English to condemn them. In an earlier time, a French manuscript of the fourteenth century shows an Irish noble horseman clad in archaic coat of mail with no stirrups and bare feet. That Irish cavalry held their spears overarm rather than couched underarm is also a primitive military custom, reminiscent of ancient Celtic horsemen hurling spears before their initial contact. This, however, is the most effective tactic of light cavalrymen determined to harass and avoid confrontation.

In battle, records John Dymmok, 'every horseman hath two or three horses, and to every horse a knave; his horse of service is always led spare, and his knave, which carrieth his harness [*armour*] and spear [*presumably spears*], rideth upon the other, or else upon a hackney.' The lowest in status of the three main contingents of Irish armies was the kern. 'The kern is a kind of footman, slightly armed with a sword, a target of wood [*shield*], or a bow and sheaf of arrows with barbed heads, or else three darts [*javelins*], which they cast with wonderful facility and nearness, a weapon more noisome to the enemy, especially horsemen, than it is deadly; within these few years they have practised the musket and caliver, and are grown good and ready shot.' Earlier, Sir Anthony St Leger described these light foot-soldiers as 'naked men, but only for their shirts and small coats. And they have darts and short bows; which sort of people be both hardy and active to search woods or morasses, in the which they be hard to be beaten.'

The ferocity of the kerns left deep impressions on many veterans of the Irish wars. In 1600, Gervase Markham wrote a poem in which he imagined the town of Kerne as an Irish Sodom. Because of the licentious behaviour of its inhabitants, it is drowned beneath the waters of Lough Erne and the citizens transformed into wolves.

> The kerns sprung thus from this prodigious brood
> Are still as lewd as when their city stood.
> Fraught with all vice, replete with villainy,
> They still rebel and that most treacherously.
> Like brutish Indians these wild Irish live;
> Their quiet neighbours they delight to grieve.
> Cruel and bloody, barbarous and rude,
> Dire vengeance at their heels hath them pursued.
> They are the savagest of all the nation;
> Amongst them out I made my peregrination,
> Where many wicked customs I did see
> Such as all honest hearts I hope will flee.

From the verse above, it can be seen that by the sixteenth century the gulf in understanding between Irish and English cultures had become irreconcilable. The disdain of Giraldus had been succeeded by the invective of Tudor conquest.

The Irish of the sixteenth century were as adept at guerilla warfare as their forefathers. 'Because they are only trained to skirmish upon bogs and difficult passes or passages of woods,' observed Fynes Moryson in 1600, 'and not to stand or fight in a firm body upon the plains, they think it no shame to fly or run off from fighting, as they advantage.' 'A flying enemy,' is how Edmund Spencer chose to describe the Irish warrior's tactics. 'Hiding himself in woods and bogs, from whence he will not draw forth but into some strait passage or perilous ford where he knows the army [*of the enemy*] must needs pass, there will he lie in wait, and if he find advantage fit, will dangerously hazard the troubled soldier.' Right into the sixteenth century, the Irish maintained a particularly Celtic manner of warfare: light cavalry and guerilla tactics. It was to prove relentless and costly for the English.

Gaelic culture was predominant among the native Irish and the Anglo-Irish, more so than in any other Celtic realm. The language was spoken throughout the land and even in the Pale, while Gaelic law was still an institution difficult for the English to comprehend. 'For whereas by the just and honourable law of England, murder, manslaughter, rape, robbery, and theft are punished with death, by the Irish custom, or Brehon Law, the highest of these offences was punished only by fine, which they called an ericke.' Such humanity was not appreciated by the English and featured little in their savage dealings with the Irish in war. Leading Irishmen continued to elect their leaders in the time-honoured Celtic manner. 'It is a custom amongst all the Irish that presently after the death of any of their chief Lords or Captains, they do presently assemble themselves to a place generally appointed and known unto them, to choose another in his stead: where they do nominate and elect for the most part not the eldest son nor any of the children of their Lord deceased, but the next to him of blood that is the eldest and worthiest.' Again, such good sense was not appreciated by the English who had fought many wars over the rights of the elder son to claim his father's throne.

Once the English had reconstructed royal authority after the Wars of the Roses, the Tudor dynasty set about curbing the prevailing Gaelic culture of Ireland. In 1494, Henry VII issued Poyning's Law which dictated that the Irish Parliament could only pass bills approved by the Privy Council in London. It ensured a subordinate, colonial role for the Irish government and was only repealed in 1782. Next was an attack on Irish customs. Henry VIII struck at the very heart of Gaelic identity when he recommended a ban on native appearance. 'No person or persons shall be shorn, or shaven above the ears, or use the wearing of hair called glibes [*a thick fringe of hair on the forehead that frequently covered the eyes and was characteristic of Irish warriors*], or have to use any hair growing upon their upper lips, called or named a crommeal [*an attack on the moustache, the quintessence of Celtic manhood for so long*], or to use or wear any shirt, kerchief, of linen cap, coloured or dyed with saffron [*the traditional colour of Irish noblemen*], nor yet to use or wear in any of their shirts or smocks above 7 yards of cloth. Be it enacted that every person or persons, the King's true subjects, in habiting this land of Ireland, of what estate, condition or degree he or they be, or shall be, to the uttermost of their power, cunning, and knowledge, shall use and speak commonly the English tongue and language.'

The prohibition of Irish manners and customs was made law in the reign of Queen Elizabeth in 1571. 'The sons of all husbandmen and ploughmen shall follow the same occupation as their fathers. If the son of a husbandman or ploughman will become a kern, galloglas, or horseboy, or will take any other idle trade of life, he shall be imprisoned for a twelve month and fined.' Private armies were banned. 'For avoiding of robberies and idleness, no lords or any others shall keep more horsemen or footmen than they are able to maintain upon their own costs. They shall present the names of such men as they keep in a book to the justices of the peace in the country where they dwell.' Failure to do so brought death. 'All Irish law called the Brehon Law to be of no force, and all persons taking upon them to adjudge causes according to the said law, to have a twelve months' imprisonment and to forfeit all their goods and chattels.' The wearing of Irish clothes and the Gaelic hairstyle known as the glib was to be punished with a £100 fine. Such measures may seem silly or impossible to maintain, but it was a law against Irishness and meant that every Irishman had been declared an outlaw. This was a convenient weapon against rebels, if no other crime could be proved.

Gaelic discontent with the Tudor anglicisation of Ireland was strongest in western Ulster. Beyond the river Bann and Lough Neagh was a land ringed by mountains and deep cut waterways, a land the Normans had never penetrated. Gaelic clans ruled the territory as they had for centuries and the

An Irish lord, probably a MacSwiney of a galloglas dynasty, prepares to set out on a cattle-raid. From a woodcut, probably by John Derricke, for his book *The Image of Irelande*, published in London in 1581.

English counter-attack against the cattle-raiders and the Irish chieftain is wounded. From John Derricke's *The Image of Irelande*.

O'Neills were, as always, the dominant family. But, even there, the foreign policy of Henry VIII cracked open splits in the Celtic society. The head of the O'Donnels of Donegal submitted to the English king and he was followed by Con O'Neill who pledged the loyalty of Tyrone, forsook the title of The O'Neill, and agreed to pursue English customs and language. Such submission meant that Con O'Neill's eldest son, Matthew, was his successor according to the English law of primogeniture. This was too much for another of Con O'Neill's sons, Shane. He had been elected successor by the senior members of the clan according to Brehon law and the principle of tanistry. He set about proving he was the more effective man. Matthew was proclaimed a bastard son, ambushed and murdered. Con O'Neill was thrown out of Tyrone, dying shortly after in the Pale. Fifteen thousand Scots mercenaries were invited over from Kintyre and Islay: the Campbells, McLeans, MacLeods and McKays. In addition, Shane broke with the tradition that only freemen could carry weapons: all the peasants on his estates were armed. The Anglo-Irish army in the Pale barely numbered 2,000 and were clearly over-awed, preferring to sit tight and observe Shane consolidate his power.

In 1561, Shane O'Neill moved against his biggest rivals in Ulster. Calvach O'Donnel was betrayed by his wife to Shane. He kept O'Donnel in chains and his woman as a mistress. All of Ulster was now under his direct control. The Earl of Sussex, Lord Lieutenant of Ireland, had to act. But Shane was in no need of a confrontation. Sussex advanced to Armagh in south east Ulster and Shane's lightly armed warriors kept out of his way. The English army paraded on through Tyrone to Lough Foyle. They captured 4,000 cattle but not even this traditional challenge could bring O'Neill into the field. Eventually, achieving nothing, the English force wearied of the guerilla response and backed off to Newry. Tyrone had been ravaged but the hearts and minds of the Ulstermen were with O'Neill. In order to put his case fairly to Queen Elizabeth, Shane accepted an offer of safe conduct and travelled to London.

To the English, Ireland was one of the frontiers of Europe, a land on the edge of their world, full of barbarians. It is little surprising then that the courtiers of Elizabethan London observed O'Neill's retainers with 'as much wonder as if they had come from China or America,' according to a contemporary chronicler. Indeed, the Celtic party, headed by The O'Neill, presented a fantastic sight. In defiance of previous Tudor legislation, his warriors were wholly Gaelic in appearance. Their hair was long: fringes hanging down to cover their eyes. They wore shirts with large sleeves dyed with saffron, short tunics and shaggy cloaks. Some walked with bare feet, others wore leather sandals. The galloglas carried battle-axes and wore long coats of mail. O'Neill was himself a man of fearsome reputation. He could not abide anything English. He is said to have hanged a warrior for eating an English biscuit and called a stronghold 'Fuath-na-Gall', 'hatred of the Englishmen'.

Though bold and confident, O'Neill was not foolish. In front of Elizabeth, he begged for forgiveness for his alleged rebellion and explained his case. Matthew O'Neill had been a mere bastard, so, according to both English and Celtic laws of succession, Shane was entitled to be The O'Neill. Above all, the O'Neills had run Ulster as long as anyone could remember. But Shane was willing to admit Elizabeth's overlordship and help her in any way possible. The Queen held back her anger and invited him to clear eastern Ulster of the 'robbers of Hebrides': the military Scots families who had settled in Antrim. Thus, O'Neill returned to Ireland with his status enhanced, his position recognised, and carte blanche to acquire further territory in north-east Ireland.

The MacDonalds were the chief galloglas family of Antrim. They were the sons of the Lord of Islay and Kintyre and great-great-grandsons of John MacDonald of the Isles. Arming his warriors with matchlock handguns, O'Neill saw no need to employ the hit-and-run tactics he had against the English, but chose confrontation. The MacDonalds in their turn raised the alarm for reinforcements from the Western Isles by lighting beacons on the coastal cliffs of Antrim. They clashed a few miles south of Ballycastle. The battle was ferocious and long. By nightfall, it was clear that the O'Neills were victorious. The leading MacDonalds were made prisoner and thirteen clan banners captured. Queen Elizabeth rejoiced at the breaking of the Scots foothold in Ireland, but now she faced an independent Irish warlord of even greater strength. O'Neill followed up his military victories with political strategy. He wrote to the king of France requesting 6,000 troops 'to assist in expelling the English'. O'Neill was under no illusions. He played along with Elizabeth's efforts to set one Gaelic faction against another, but he knew that in the end it was the English who were his greatest enemy.

In 1566, Sir Henry Sidney, a new English Lord Deputy of Ireland, set about curbing the power of The O'Neill. 'Lucifer was never more puffed up with pride and ambition than O'Neill is,' he wrote to Elizabeth. 'He continually keepeth six hundred armed men about him and is able to bring into the field one thousand horsemen and four thousand foot. He is the only strong man of Ireland.' Marching to the mouth of the river Blackwater, Sidney captured O'Neill's Coney Island stronghold in Lough Neagh. A stone tower 30 feet high and surrounded by sharpened stakes, a thick hedge, ditch, and stone rampart, it was the Ulsterman's treasury. Sidney then progressed through Tyrone, again demonstrating English power, and again being avoided by O'Neill's men who had reverted to their guerilla tactics. Such a parade of strength, however, had damaged Shane's pride and purse and restored the O'Donnells in Donegal. With little money to pay his followers and a dent in his control of the land, O'Neill had to act decisively or he would lose the support of his warriors. He decided to regain his reputation as a winner by attacking the O'Donnells.

In the spring of 1567, the O'Neills rode into view of the O'Donnells at Farsetmore, a sandy ford across the river Swilly. At first, the horsemen of both vanguards exchanged blows. Spears were thrown over-arm in the traditional Celtic manner. But the clatter of javelins was joined by the crack of gun-fire as the arquebusiers of each side joined in. The O'Donnells were pushed back to their prepared positions on boggy ground. Reinforced by galloglas of the clan MacSwiney, they then counter-attacked. Galloglas of the MacDonalds fought alongside the O'Neills. 'Fierce and desperate were the grim and terrible looks that each cast at the other out of their starlike eyes,' recorded the *Annals of the Four Masters*. 'They raised the battle-cry aloud and their united shouting when rushing together was sufficient to strike with dismay and turn to flight the feeble and unwarlike. They proceeded to strike and cut down one another for a long time, so that men were soon laid low, youths slain, and robust heroes mangled in the slaughter.' The galloglas of both sides, axes swinging, were engaged in a struggle fuelled not by the animosity of their pay-masters but by deeply inbred clan rivalry. Exhaustion brought the battle to its crisis and the O'Neills were the first to break. Many tried to cross the river Swilly, but the waters had risen since they first crossed and many were drowned.

Shane O'Neill's forces were routed and with them disappeared his power. His judgement shaken by the defeat, Shane sought shelter among the MacDonalds of Antrim. Although politics had united them while Shane was riding high, the Scots clan could not forget the damage he had done to their people on behalf of Elizabeth. Initially, they welcomed him and helped him forget his sorrows with a drinking party. But, whether it was the drink or a prepared trap, fighting broke out. Shane and his bodyguard were cut to pieces. A few days later, O'Neill's head was presented to Sir Henry Sidney. Where the English had failed, Celtic warriors had succeeded in destroying the one Irish warlord who could have kept at least one part of Ireland wholly Gaelic. In 1569, the title of O'Neill and the sovereignty of the dynasty was abolished. The Elizabethan conquest had begun in earnest.

Frontier warfare brings out the worst in its warriors. Both sides consider each other alien and inhuman, so savagery prevails. Beyond the Pale, English conquistadors suspended any humanity they possessed and treated the Irish as they would the Indians of America: natives to be dispossessed and exterminated. The Irish responded with equal ferocity. The English spearheaded their campaigns with warlords of barbaric renown. In 1570, Humphrey Gilbert was made commander of the English army of Munster. Any visitor to his camp was compelled to walk between two lines of severed Irish heads leading to his tent. Largely due to the efforts of Gilbert, resistance in Munster was crushed and the land divided into English plantations. Similar ruthlessness ensured the English conquest of Connacht. Only Ulster remained a Celtic realm. And yet its leading Gaelic heir of The O'Neill had been educated in England as a potential weapon against the Irish.

Hugh O'Neill was the son of Matthew, the son of Con O'Neill. After the

Homage by the citizens of Dublin to Sir Henry Sidney, Lord Deputy of Ireland, after he returns from a victory over the Gaelic Irish in 1575. From John Derricke's *The Image of Irelande*.

O Sydney worthy of tryple re.
nowne,
For plagyng the traytours that
troubled the crowne. 1581.

125

murder of his father by Shane O'Neill, Hugh was brought up in England as a royal ward. Attached to the household of the Earl of Leicester, he learned lessons in England, both political and military, which were to prove highly useful. Returning to Ireland in the year after Shane O'Neill's death, he served with the government forces. He was considered safe enough to be rewarded with the title of Earl of Tyrone. The English now had a puppet ruler of Ulster through whom they could further exploit the country; or so they thought. Once settled in his homeland, Hugh's Gaelic blood rose. He consolidated his native power base. 'All men of rank within the province are become his men,' it was observed, 'they receive his wages and promise him service according to the usual manner of that country.' In 1593, Hugh O'Neill was elected by his clan to the title of The O'Neill. It was a slap in the face of English law. Drawn between both the role of an English peer and that of a Gaelic chieftain, it was to the latter that Hugh finally dedicated his life. Such a turn of events was encouraged by the presence of Red Hugh O'Donnell. Having dramatically escaped from Dublin castle, O'Donnell gathered his forces, including 3,000 Scots mercenaries, and took his revenge on the English colonists in Connacht: 'sparing no male between fifteen and sixty years old who was unable to speak Irish.'

O'Neill was ordered to attack O'Donnell, which he did, but he also dragged his feet. Observing the English hard-pressed, he continued to build up his own forces. Queen Elizabeth had permitted him 600 troops, trained by English captains. These were then used to train further recruits: Irish

Spanish morion helmet of around 1580. The Irish obtained much arms and armour from abroad, usually smuggled through English ports and sometimes direct from Spain.

and Scots mercenaries called bonaghts. The institution of the galloglas had declined since the heroic days of the early sixteenth century. Many of the Scots adventurer families had long since become a part of the Irish community. They were landowners and no longer needed to fight for their living. Effective English fleets in the Irish Sea prevented any frequent forays from the Western Isles. Besides, the traditional arms of the galloglas, the sword and pole-axe, had been supplanted by the pike and musket as the universal instruments of death. Those Scots warriors who now fought with the Irish mainly served under the name of bonaghts and wielded pike or musket. Organised in companies of 100 men and armed with the latest weapons imported from Scotland and Spain, or smuggled from English ports, there was little to distinguish them from their English adversaries, apart from the drone of the bagpipe that urged them on into battle.

By 1595, O'Neill had recruited and trained some 1,000 pikemen, 4,000 musketeers, and 1,000 cavalry. He was strong enough to declare his Gaelic interests and was forthwith proclaimed a traitor. An English policing force was mauled at Clontibret. The O'Donnells captured Sligo, thus securing the south-west approach to Ulster against English reinforcements. But, before all-out war could break, a truce was called. In the meantime, O'Neill asked for assistance from England's arch enemy—Spain. In his correspondence, he allied the survival of Gaelic Ireland with the re-establishing of the Catholic religion against the Protestant regime of Elizabeth. He received a friendly ear but effective military aid was not forthcoming. No agreement was reached between O'Neill and the English and, in 1597, a three-pronged campaign was launched against Ulster. Each element was repulsed and O'Neill and O'Donnell were forced ever closer in the common defence of their land.

In 1598, Sir Henry Bagenal of Newry was instructed to relieve an English fortress on the banks of the river Blackwater besieged by the Ulstermen. He commanded an army of around 4,000 foot and 300 horse. Almost 2,000 of these were raw recruits, barely a couple of months in Ireland and poorly equipped. 'The want of the men's apparel is such,' wrote Captain Francis Stafford, 'that if they be not speedily relieved, many will march without shoes or stockings.' Irish clothing was recommended for the English soldiers as being cheaper and more durable than the clothing imported from England, but Lord Burgh, Lord Deputy of Ireland, could not accept this because such clothing was made by the Irish who would thus receive 'her Majesty's good coin, wherewith they buy out of Denmark, Scotland and other parts, powder and munition to maintain their rebellion.' The rest of Bagenal's army, however, were veterans of the Irish war, half of which were probably native Irishmen, including many cavalry.

The English force marched from Armagh to the Blackwater across 'hard and hilly ground, within caliver shot of wood and bog on both sides, which was wholly possessed by the enemy continually playing upon us.' Charles Montague, Lieutenant-General of the English, was correct in this account.

O'Neill and O'Donnell had invested some 5,000 warriors in the densely-forested countryside. The English marched in battle order, returning the skirmishing fire, but inevitably the advancing line became strung out and soon it was to be every man for himself. The English pressed on; the fort on the Blackwater was now nearer than Armagh. But O'Neill had carefully prepared the territory. Brushwood and undergrowth had been weaved together to create living fences. Pits had been dug to ensnare the unweary and impede cavalry action. Finally, boggy land was linked by a trench some five feet deep and four feet over, with a thorny hedge on the other side.

The English tried to break through. Their formations were scattered. The first half of the English vanguard was isolated beyond the trench, within sight of the beleaguered garrison of the Blackwater. The garrison threw up their caps in joy and dashed out to meet the English relief force. But O'Neill was well in command of the situation and pulled the noose tight. His skirmishers pummelled the English ranks further. Then horsemen surged forward and foot-soldiers armed with sword and shield. This was not a time for orthodox pike and shot tactics. Irish blades cut in among the English. The recent recruits broke before the Irish war cries. The vanguard was cut to pieces.

Realising the danger of his vanguard, Bagenal rode forward to support them. At the trench, he raised the visor of his helmet to gain a better view. Gun shot shattered his face and killed him instantly. The other English commanders decided on retreat, but this was easier said than done. A loud explosion ripped through the chaos. An English musketeer had gone to replenish his powder-flask: his lighted match carelessly sparked over the open powder barrels and the contents blew up, throwing a black cloud over the disintegrating army. Confusion tore the English apart. Some had not received the orders of retreat and pressed on to the killing ground of the trench. Others threw down their arms and deserted into the woods. At the end of the day, a shocked and bewildered English army reached Armagh. O'Neill had won a great victory. He did not follow it up: the remnants of the English army were allowed to escape. But Ulster remained resolutely Gaelic until the end of the century.

The strength of Hugh O'Neill's military leadership lay in his combination of professional training and the latest weapons with a traditional Celtic talent for guerilla warfare. In his victory he showed that Gaelic warriors, given the arms and training, were more than a match for any contemporary army. This is worth stressing, as much has been written about the archaic nature of Irish warfare and Celtic warfare in general. Certainly, it was a hard fact realised by English officers at the time. 'The Irish are most ready, well disciplined,' said one, 'and as good marksmen as France, Flanders, or Spain can show.' The Elizabethan invasion of Ireland was not so much an act of colonial discipline as a full-blown continental war, and one in which the Gaelic Irish won much success.

In the next century, the Irish were joined by Spanish soldiers landed at

Kinsale. Drawn out of their strong defensive situation in Ulster, the Gaelic Irish advanced to support the Spanish on the soutern coast of Munster. The English were besieging Kinsale, and O'Neill hoped to crush them against the Spanish. Advancing in the most contemporary tactical formations—the *tercio* of pike and shot—O'Neill led a formidable force. But his Celtic warriors were far away from familiar territory and were now being drawn into a confrontation on open ground. Confusion and panic broke the army. The Spanish and Irish did not act together. The English triumphed and O'Neill dismally dragged his forces back to Ulster. The Spanish capitulated and sailed home. A great opportunity had been lost. The Gaelic Irish had taken the offensive in what could have been a final shattering blow to English occupation. Instead, it proved the downfall of the Gaelic regime.

The English pressed hard on O'Neill and a harsh winter in 1603 finally compelled the Celtic warlord to surrender. Queen Elizabeth was dead but James I continued the anglicization of Ireland. O'Neill was allowed to return to his Ulster estates, but it was no longer a Celtic realm. English law predominated. Gaelic laws and customs were illegal. English government effectively reduced the power of the Gaelic chieftains; so much so that O'Neill and O'Donnell felt the land had now become alien and they preferred to sail into exile. O'Neill died in Rome in 1616. There would be further uprisings against the English and the O'Neill dynasty was far from finished, but essentially Gaelic power had been broken. The culture remained, but the military potential of Celtic warriors to maintain an independent realm was over. The same was true of other Celtic regions.

In Wales, the fiery independence of the Celtic Welsh was paradoxically undermined by the victory of one of its warlords. In 1485, Henry Tudor, a

Caricatured Irish soldiers in the service of Gustavus Aldolphus, 1631. From a contemporary German Broadside now in the British Museum, London. After the Elizabethan conquest, many Irish warriors sort a better life abroad.

In folchem Habit Gehen die 800 In Stettin angekommen Irrlander oder Irren.

member of the Anglesey dynasty, sailed to England under the red dragon standard. He advanced with a Welsh army to the battle of Bosworth. There, he smashed an English army, killed an English king, and assumed the English crown. At the time, a Venetian ambassador proclaimed that the Welsh had at last regained their liberty. But, in reality, this was not a Welsh victory, it was a Tudor triumph. The Tudor dynasty could not afford to tolerate any independent powers that might threaten its security. So Wales was incorporated into a union under the English crown. The old tripartite Wales of Celtic, Marcher and Royal estates was reorganised as English counties. The Welsh language was banned from public life. It was relegated to the language of the common people: no longer spoken by ambitious intelligentsia or the ruling classes. That this Celtic cultural defeat was delivered by an English monarch with Welsh blood in his veins seems to have softened the blow, for there were no more armed uprisings. Perhaps the Welsh felt they could claim with satisfaction that they were now ruled by a Welshman. Certainly, the Tudors rewarded their Welsh followers and could depend on their support.

In Scotland, English was also the language of the rulers, with Celtic the tongue of the ruled. However, after centuries of fighting the English for their independence, Scots aristocrats were far from happy to be told they were speaking the language of their enemy. Therefore, in the fifteenth century, the northern English spoken by the Scots ruling class became known as Scots, while the previously Scots Gaelic language was termed Irish. A wedge was again hammered between the anglicized Scots and the Gaelic Scots during the Reformation. Scots rulers accepted Protestant ideas and were urged to crush old Gaelic affinities to the Catholic faith, thus further lessening the presence of Celtic culture in Scotland. By 1521, the divide between the Gaelic Highlands and the Scots of the Lowlands was crystallised in a characterisation that has lingered on ever since.

'Just as among the Scots we find two distinct tongues,' wrote John Major in his *History of Greater Britain,*' so we likewise find two different ways of life and conduct. For some are born in the forests and mountains of the north, and these we call men of the Highland, but the others men of the Lowland. By foreigners the former are called Wild Scots, the latter householding Scots. One half of Scotland speaks Irish and all of these as well as the Islanders we reckon to belong to the Wild Scots. In dress, in the manner of their outward life, and in good morals, for example, these come behind the householding Scots—yet they are not less, but rather much more, prompt to fight. It is, however, with the householding Scots that the government and direction of the kingdom is to be found. One part of the Wild Scots have a wealth of cattle, sheep, and horses, and these with a thought for the possible loss of their possessions yield more willing obedience to the courts of law and the king. The other part of these people delight in the chase and a life of indolence. Their chieftains eagerly follow bad men if only they may not have the need to labour. They are full of

131

mutual dissensions and war rather than peace is their normal condition. The Scottish kings have with difficulty been able to withstand the inroads of these men. These men hate our householding Scots, on account of their differing speech, as much as they do the English.'

Although this description of the Gaelic Scots by an outsider is a typical example of anti-Celtic propaganda, it nevertheless demonstrates the independent lifestyle maintained by the Gaelic clans and their clashes with Lowland kings. For, throughout the fifteenth century, the Gaelic lords of the Western Isles and Highlands were as much a danger to the kings of Scotland as the English. Indeed, many of the island chieftains used alliances with English factions to pursue their clan ambitions. The leading dynasty throughout this period was the MacDonalds. All other island clans did homage to them: the MacLeans of Mull, the MacLeods of Skye, the MacNeils of Barra, the MacIntoshes and the MacKinnons. In 1411, Donald, Lord of the Isles, led a formidable army to within a few miles of Aberdeen. In 1429, Alexander, Lord of the Isles, sacked Inverness. In 1451, John, Lord of the Isles, seized the royal castles of Urquhart, Inverness and Ruthven, and ravaged the islands in the Firth of Clyde. In 1491, Alexander, a nephew of the Lord of the Isles, invaded Ross and destroyed the castle of Inverness. It is little wonder, then, that when James IV ascended the throne in 1488 his immediate attention was directed towards the Islands and Highlands.

'The king is of noble stature, neither tall nor short, and as handsome in complexion and shape as a man can be.' So wrote Don Pedro de Ayala, Spanish ambassador, of James IV. 'He speaks the following foreign languages: Latin very well; French, German, Flemish, Italian, and Spanish. The king speaks besides, the language of the savages who live in some parts of Scotland and on the islands. He is courageous, even more so than a king should be. I have seen him often undertake most dangerous things in the last wars. He is not a good captain, because he begins to fight before he has given his orders.' Armed thus with both an aggressive nature and a working knowledge of Gaelic, James sailed to the island strongholds of the clans and commanded their respect. James was the last monarch to speak Gaelic and he used it to good effect. He treated the Highland chieftains with friendship and granted them land. In return, the clansmen acknowledged his overlordship. James even extended his influence over the Irish Sea, receiving the submission of Hugh O'Donnell of western Ulster.

The Celtic warriors confronted by James on his expeditions to the Western Isles have been described by John Major. 'From the mid-leg to the foot, they go uncovered. Their dress, for an over-garment, is a loose plaid and a shirt dyed with saffron. They are armed with bow and arrows, a broadsword, and a small halberd. They always carry in their belt a stout dagger, single-edged, but of the sharpest. In time of war they cover the whole body with a coat of mail, made of iron rings, and in it they fight. The common folk among the Wild Scots go out to battle with the whole body clad in a linen garment sewed together in patchwork, well daubed with wax or with pitch, and with an over-coat of deerskin.' After a few years of settlement, it was inevitable that the clansmen should kick against royal authority.

At the age of 25, James revoked all the charters he had granted the lords of the Isles. It was a constitutional act, but it now meant that the clansmen were tenants at the king's pleasure. To secure this relationship he appointed several deputies over the region once ruled by the Lord of the Isles. Displeased by this increased supervision of their traditional spheres of power, the clansmen became restless; particularly so when one of the king's deputies, the Earl of Argyll, was noted to grant favours to his own clan members. In the tenseness of the situation, James imprisoned Donald Owre, the generally acknowledged successor to the last Lord of the Isles. Later, James relented and released him. It was to be a costly generosity. At once, Donald set about claiming his true right of lordship. Many disaffected chieftains joined his banner, including MacLean of Lochbuie, MacLean of Duart, and Ewen Allanson of Lochiel. Supporters of the king in the Isles were killed and clansmen ravaged Bute.

In retaliation, the Scots parliament enacted several laws against the independent Celtic warriors. The king's muscle was supplied by one of his deputies, the Earl of Huntly, who assaulted clan strongholds on the mainland, and the king's ships which sailed for the remote castle of Cairn na Burgh to the west of Mull. Little is known of the action in this confrontation, but it is clear the Highlanders were not quelled. Further ships were equipped with cannons and German gunners from Edinburgh Castle and these patrolled the Western Isles. By 1507, however, the last rebel stronghold was besieged by the royal fleet and Donald Owre had been captured. Relationships between the clansmen and the king became more friendly, but the extent of James' trust of the Highlanders is demonstrated by his strengthening of several castles at strategic points throughout the Highlands. It might seem that James had maintained his authority, but in reality little had been achieved against the Gaelic Scots. The clansmen remained semi-independent warlords ready to prove a major threat to Scots kings in the future.

By 1511, James had other enemies to consider. Scotland was enmeshed in continental affairs. Her Auld Alliance with the king of France was tested as the Pope, the king of Spain, the Doge, the Emperor, and the king of England all prepared to divide France. The Scots stood by their traditional ally and in 1513 James demanded Henry VIII withdraw from his invasion of France. Henry refused, adding that he was 'the very owner of Scotland' which James 'held of him by homage', thus evoking the claims of English kings before the war of Independence. Outraged, James responded by recruiting a great army and marching across the Tweed. Raiders rode ahead, clashing with the border landlords and their retinues. In the main body of the army, seventeen cannon were dragged forward by four hundred oxen. Three

English castles fell to James, but many Scotsmen had already lost the stomach for fighting and desertion plagued the king's army. To march on York was now considered foolhardy and unnecessary. The invasion slowed down. An English army was reported to be advancing northwards. Led by the Earl of Surrey, it numbered about 20,000. The Scots army cannot have differed greatly in strength as neither side was daunted by the numbers of the other. James prepared a secure position on Flodden Hill and awaited confrontation.

The rain rushed down the hillsides around Flodden, overflowing streams and transforming fields into swamps. James felt content with the situation. If the English attacked, his cannon and schiltrons would hurl them back down the slippery slopes of Flodden Hill. If they did not, then he could retreat to the frontier and reinforce his army for whatever move he considered prudent. Surrey tried to draw James off the hill with a challenge to come down from his fortress-like position and fight on the plain of Milfield. But, though a lover of the tournament and the chivalric duel, James refused: 'Show to the Earl of Surrey that it beseemeth him not, being an Earl, so largely to attempt a great prince. His Grace will take and hold his ground at his own pleasure.' James was a cooler general than Ayala had credited him for. Surrey, however, was no fool either. He commanded his troops to march northwards and then wheel round so as to stand between the Scots and Scotland. The next day, James awoke to this danger. He had to get to Branxton Hill, to the north-west of Flodden, before the English, otherwise they would possess a similarly impregnable position. The alarm was sounded. The camp was stripped down and burnt: a great cloud of smoke hung over the land. Teams of oxen heaved the Scots' cannon across to Branxton Hill. Battle was approaching and the Scots assembled in their familiar schiltrons. Four massive squares took shape: the king commanded the right centre while the majority of Gaelic warriors in the army—the Highlanders and Islanders—formed the right wing. A further body of soldiers were placed in reserve. They now all looked down the muddy slopes of Branxton Hill at the advancing English.

The Earl of Surrey felt distinctly uneasy. The Scots had moved quicker than anticipated, leaving the English vanguard in the deadground at the base of the hill awaiting the rest of the army. If the Scots had attacked then, they could have destroyed the English piecemeal. Instead, time passed, and the English rearguard joined its fellow soldiers. At last, the Scots' cannon opened fire, hurling balls of stone among the enemy. The English replied with their guns. Apparently, the English gunners were more accurate and their shot crashed into James' division, mowing down his armour-plated comrades. It was then that James' bold recklessness finally took over from his strategic prudence and he led his warriors forward. Before the advancing schiltrons, the English right flank just ran away. But the English counter-attacked and both backed off. The king of Scotland's division surged on towards the Earl of Surrey. It was in this combat in the centre

Scots sword of the type known as a claymore, or claidheanih-mor. Early sixteenth-century, now in the British Museum, London.

that the battle was won and lost. Thomas Ruthall, the bishop of Durham, described the crucial conflict only a few weeks later. 'The Scots were so surely harnessed that the shot of arrows did them no harm and when it came to hand strokes of bills and halberds, they were so mighty that they would not fall when struck by four or five bills all at once. But our bills did us more good that day than bows for they soon disappointed the Scots of their long spears. And when they came to hand strike, the Scots fought valiantly with their swords yet were unable to resist the bills which alighted on them so thickly.' From contemporary accounts, it appears the English soldiers armed with 8-foot bills, a kind of pole-arm, were at an advantage in close combat as the Scots' 15-foot spears were too unwieldly to be effective. Yet when the Scots threw them down and drew their swords, they were outreached by the bills.

In the struggling crowd, James also threw aside his pike, slashing and hacking at the English with his sword. He got within a spear's length of Surrey, but a series of bill blows cut him down. It might be thought that the death of a commander would go unnoticed in the chaos of fighting, but unless he is always on show, urging his warriors forward, the loss is soon clear and the fight drains from soldiers only there because of him. At the foot of Branxton Hill, the death of James broke his army. A further surprise appearance of an English force around the hillside shattered the Highlanders who had yet to prove themselves but saw little reason for standing in the dusk with no king to note their loyalty. In the fading light, the surviving Scots made their way home, pursued relentlessly by the victorious English.

The death of James IV, the last Gaelic-speaking monarch, did not particularly harm the Celtic cause in Scotland. Indeed, his death initiated a century of uncertainty and weakness for the Scots monarchy that allowed the Highland warlords to increase their power and liberty. Again they allied themselves with the Tudors, but in the end victory for the English could mean only ultimate defeat for all Scots. For with the increasing influence of English Protestantism on Scotland and its eventual success, the Catholic-orientated culture of Gaelic Scotland was dealt a severe blow. Yet, in 1603, it was the Scots' king James VI who became James I of England and succeeded Elizabeth, that scourge of Celtic society. Like the Welsh, over a century earlier, all Scots could at least claim that Britain was ruled by one of their own. But here again, as with the Tudors, dynastic survival overcame national loyalty and James VI came down hard on the clans.

In the year of James I's accession, a bloody incident at Glenfruin encouraged a stern anti-Gaelic stance. In a pitched battle between the Macgregors and the Colquhouns of Luss, two hundred of the Colquhouns and several spectating citizens from Dumbarton were slaughtered, Immediately, James passed an act outlawing the entire Macgregor clan. A few years later in 1609, James enacted further statutes against the Highlanders intended to bring them in line with the Lowlanders. One of the statutes

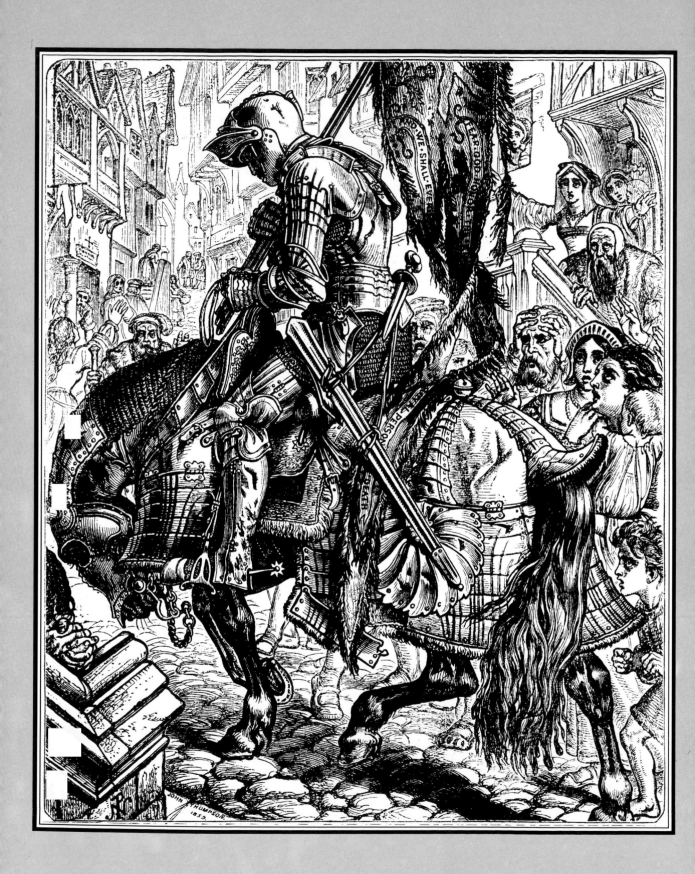

A Scots knight broken in spirit returns from the battlefield of Flodden. Aside from the death of James IV, 12 earls, 14 lords, one archbishop, three bishops, 68 knights, and 10,000 Scotsmen were killed in the battle. A composition by John Thompson, 1859, for Cassell's *British Battles on Land and Sea*.

prohibited the importation of whisky, known as *aqua vitae*, to the Western Isles. It was claimed that 'one of the special causes of the great poverty of the Isles and of the great cruelty and inhuman barbarity which has been practised by sundry of the inhabitants upon their natural friends and neighbours has been their extraordinary drinking of strong wines and aqua vitae brought in among them, partly by merchants of the mainland and partly by traffickers among themselves.' Another statute hit harder at Gaelic identity. 'The Irish language which is one of the chief and principal causes of the continuance of barbarity and incivility among the inhabitants of the Isles and Highlands may be abolished and removed.' It was decreed that every gentleman must send his eldest son or daughter to the Lowlands to learn to speak, read and write English. It was clear the English and Lowland government were intent on extinguishing the Gaelic culture of Scotland as far as it could be seen to be a political threat.

The importance of language to the identity of a people cannot be overestimated. In the ancient world, it was only the common Celtic tongue that gave unity to an otherwise varied and often divided people. The Celt existed through his language. Without it, he ceased to be truly Celtic. Thus, by ensuring Celtic was spoken only by the common people and not by their leaders, it effectively struck away at Celtic power. The destruction of their language was the greatest blow Celtic warriors could ever receive. It denied their very existence.

Bibliography

THIS IS, OF NECESSITY, A SELECT BIBLIOGRAPHY OF
BOTH PRIMARY AND SECONDARY REFERENCES

PRIMARY SOURCES

ALL THESE TEXTS ARE AVAILABLE IN ENGLISH TRANSLATIONS IN SEVERAL
EDITIONS.

Annals of Ulster: Medieval Irish history from the earliest times.

Appian, *Roman History*: principal source for Roman conquest of Spain by a
Graeco-Roman of the second century AD.

John Barbour, *The Bruce*: fourteenth-century poem about Robert Bruce
written by the Archdeacon of Aberdeen.

Brut Y Tywysogion—Chronicle of the Princes: Welsh history of Wales from
the seventh to thirteenth centuries. There are two other versions of this
chronicle, *The Red Book of Hergest* and *The Kings of the Saxons*.

Caesar, *The Gallic War*: first century BC autobiography of campaigns against
the Celts of France.

Four Ancient Books of Wales: nineteenth-century compilation of the major
early medieval British sagas, including the Urien cycle.

Wars of the Gaedhil with the Gaill: twelfth-century Irish account of the
invasion of Ireland by the Vikings.

Gildas, *The Ruin of Britain*: sixth-century chronicle of the Anglo-Saxon
wars by a Romano-Briton from the northern kingdom of Clyde.

Giraldus Cambrensis, *Historical Works*, including a geography of Wales and
Ireland and an account of the Norman invasion of Ireland: twelfth-
century chronicles by a Norman-Welsh ecclesiastic in touch with eye-
witnesses of the events he describes.

138

The Gododdin: sixth-century poem attributed to Aneirin, a northern Briton, recounting war against the Angles.

Lanercost Chronicle: fourteenth-century chronicle by an anonymous English historian at Lanercost near Carlisle.

The Mabinogion: thirteenth-century compilation of Welsh tales and history of ancient times.

Nennius, *The History of the British*: ninth-century chronicle by a Briton.

Pausanias, *Description of Greece*: principal source for Celtic invasion of Greece by a Greek geographer of the second century AD.

Scalacronica: fourteenth-century history of the Edwardian wars in Scotland by Sir Thomas Gray, an English knight held prisoner in Edinburgh castle during the wars of Edward III.

Edmund Spenser, *A View of the Present State of Ireland*: first published in 1633, but written at the end of the sixteenth century by a Tudor Englishman.

Tain Bo Cuailnge: Irish epic tale dated to the eighth century but believed to be centuries older, perhaps pre-Christian.

SECONDARY WORKS

Alcock, L., *Arthur's Britain*, London, 1971.

Arribas, A., *The Iberians*, London, 1964.

Bannerman, J., *Studies In The History of Dalriada*, Edinburgh, 1974.

Canny, N.P., *The Elizabethan Conquest of Ireland*, Hassocks, Sussex, 1976.

Carr, A.D., 'Welshmen and the Hundred Years War', *The Welsh History Review*, Vol. 4, p.21, Cardiff, 1968.

Chadwick, H.M., *Early Scotland*, Cambridge, 1949.

Chadwick, N.K., *Early Brittany*, Cardiff, 1969.

Chadwick, N.K., *The British Heroic Age*, Cardiff, 1976.

Davies, W., *Wales In The Early Middle Ages*, Leicester, 1982.

Drinkwater, J.F., *Roman Gaul*, London, 1983.

Edwards, O.D. (editor), *Celtic Nationalism*, London, 1968.

Ellis, P.B., *Macbeth*, London, 1980.

Falls, C., *Elizabeth's Irish Wars*, London, 1950.

Filip, J., *Celtic Civilization and Its Heritage*, Prague, 1977.

Frame, R., 'The Bruces In Ireland', *Irish Historical Studies*, Vol. 19, p. 3, Dublin, 1975.

Harding, D. (editor), *Hillforts*, London, 1976.

Hatt, J-J., *Celts and Gallo-Romans*, Geneva, 1970.

Hayes-McCoy, G.A., *Irish Battles*, London, 1969.

Hogan, J., 'Shane O'Neill comes to the court of Elizabeth', *Essays and Studies presented to Professor Tadhg Ua Donnchadha*, Cork, 1947.

Hogg, A.H.A., *Hillforts of Britain*, London, 1976.

Laing, L., *The Archaeology of Late Celtic Britain and Ireland*, London, 1975.

Loyn, H.R., *The Vikings In Britain*, London, 1977.

Lydon, J., *The Lordship of Ireland In The Middle Ages*, Dublin, 1972.

Lydon, J., and MacCurtain, M., (editors), *The Gill History of Ireland* (several volumes), Dublin, 1972.

Mackie, R.L., *James IV of Scotland*, Edinburgh, 1958.

Maxwell, C., (editor), *Irish History From Contemporary Sources*, London, 1923.

McKerral, A., 'West Highland Mercenaries in Ireland', *Scottish Historical Review*, Vol. 30 p. 1, Edinburgh.

Morris, J., *The Age of Arthur*, London, 1973.

Myers, J.P. (editor), *Elizabethan Ireland: A Selection of Writings by Elizabethan Writers*, Connecticut, 1983.

Nicholson, R., *Edward III and the Scots*, Oxford, 1965.

Otway-Ruthven, A.J., *A History of Medieval Ireland*, London, 1968.

Pine, L.G., *The Highland Clans*, Newton Abbot, 1972.

Powell, T.G.E., *The Celts*, London, 1958.

Quinn, D.B., *The Elizabethans and the Irish*, Ithaca, 1966.

Rees, W., *South Wales and the March 1280–1415*, Oxford, 1924.

Sandars, H., 'The Weapons of the Iberians', *Archaeologia*, Vol. 64 p. 205, Oxford, 1913.

Scott, R.M., *Robert the Bruce*, London, 1982.

Shetelig, H., (editor) *Viking Antiquities in Great Britain and Ireland*, Oslo, 1940.

Thompson, E.A., *Saint Germanus of Auxerre and the End of Roman Britain*, Woodbridge, 1984.

Wheeler, M. and Richardson, K.M., *Hillforts of Northern France*, Oxford, 1957.

Wightman, E.M., *Gallia Belgica*, London, 1985.

Williams, A.H., *The History of Wales: The Middle Ages*, Cardiff, 1948.

PICTURE CREDITS

All colour illustrations by Angus McBride.
All black and white illustrations from Peter Newark's Historical
Pictures, except the following:
The British Museum (Pages 25, 26, 28 top, 33, 42, 51, 57, 58, 66, 135);
The National Museum of Wales, Cardiff (Pages 43, 45, 69, 90);
The National Museum of Antiquities of Scotland, Edinburgh (Page 37).

Index

Page numbers in *italics* refer to illustrations.